THE BEST KNOWN WORKS OF
W. S. GILBERT

STANDARD
THEATRE.

FIRST PRODUCTION IN THIS CITY

Of an Entirely New and Original Nautical Comic Opera,

H. M. S.

PINAFORE

COMPOSED BY ARTHUR SULLIVAN.

WRITTEN BY W. S. GILBERT.

ORIGINALLY PRODUCED AT THE "OPERA COMIQUE," LONDON, LAST MAY, AND WHERE IT IS NOW ENJOYING A MOST PROSPEROUS RUN, HAVING ALREADY BEEN PLAYED NEARLY

Three Hundred Consecutive Nights.

A. S. Seer, Theatrical Printer, 26 Union Square, New York.

AN EARLY GILBERT & SULLIVAN PROGRAM

(Courtesy of the Theatre Collection, New York Public Library)

THE BEST KNOWN WORKS

of

W. S. GILBERT

WITH THE AUTHOR'S
ILLUSTRATIONS

NEW YORK
Illustrated Editions Company
100 FIFTH AVENUE

Printed in the United States of America by
J. J. LITTLE & IVES COMPANY, NEW YORK

THE BEST KNOWN WORKS OF
W. S. GILBERT

TABLE OF CONTENTS

PUBLISHER'S NOTICE

The most popular of the light operas resulting from the collaboration of William Schwenk Gilbert and Arthur Seymour Sullivan are the three in this book, to-wit: *The Mikado, H.M.S. Pinafore,* and *The Pirates of Penzance.* It is to one of these three, produced by school and college musical organizations, that most Americans owe an acquaintance with the joyous nonsense of the Savoyards.

The wide public acquaintance with the Gilbert opera *libretti* is not matched by any similar knowledge of the *Bab Ballads,* which had made their author and illustrator famous before he met Sullivan. During the 1860's Gilbert, then a young barrister, contributed a series of verses to *Fun,* an English comic magazine, illustrated by himself over the signature BAB. The best of these are included in this book with the three operas mentioned.

For certain of the songs and arias of the operas, Gilbert later prepared illustrations in the spirit of the *Bab Ballads.* Thus we are able to publish both operas and ballads with illustrations by the author.

The Illustrated Editions Co., Inc., acknowledges with pleasure the generous help of Mr. Sylvan Baruch in the final selection of illustrations and text for this volume.

H. M. S. Pinafore

OR

THE LASS THAT LOVED A SAILOR

DRAMATIS PERSONÆ.

THE RT. HON. SIR JOSEPH PORTER, K.C.B. (*First Lord of the Admiralty*).
CAPTAIN CORCORAN (*Commanding H.M.S. Pinafore*).
TOM TUCKER (*Midshipmite*).
RALPH RACKSTRAW (*Able Seaman*).
DICK DEADEYE (*Able Seaman*).
BILL BOBSTAY (*Boatswain's Mate*).
BOB BECKET (*Carpenter's Mate*).
JOSEPHINE (*the Captain's Daughter*).
HEBE (*Sir Joseph's First Cousin*).
MRS. CRIPPS (LITTLE BUTTERCUP) (*a Portsmouth Bumboat Woman*).
   First Lord's Sisters, his Cousins, his Aunts, Sailors, Marines, etc.

SCENE.—Quarter-deck of H.M.S. *Pinafore,* off Portsmouth.
   ACT I.—Noon.   ACT II.—Night.

First produced at the Opéra Comique on May 25, 1878.

14

H. M. S. Pinafore

OR
THE LASS THAT LOVED A SAILOR

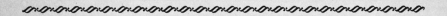

ACT ONE

SCENE.—*Quarter-deck of H.M.S. Pinafore. Sailors, led by* BOATSWAIN, *discovered cleaning brasswork, splicing rope, etc.*

CHORUS

We sail the ocean blue,
And our saucy ship's a beauty;
We're sober men and true,
And attentive to our duty.
When the balls whistle free
O'er the bright blue sea,
We stand to our guns all day;
When at anchor we ride
On the Portsmouth tide,
We have plenty of time to play.

Enter LITTLE BUTTERCUP, *with large basket on her arm.*

RECITATIVE

Hail, men-o'-war's men—safeguards of your nation,
Here is an end, at last, of all privation;
You've got your pay—spare all you can afford
To welcome Little Buttercup on board.

15

ARIA

For I'm called Little Buttercup—dear Little Buttercup,
   Though I could never tell why,
But still I'm called Buttercup—poor Little Buttercup,
   Sweet Little Buttercup I!

I've snuff and tobaccy, and excellent jacky,
   I've scissors, and watches, and knives;
I've ribbons and laces to set off the faces
   Of pretty young sweethearts and wives.

I've treacle and toffee, I've tea and I've coffee,
   Soft tommy and succulent chops;
I've chickens and conies, and pretty polonies,
   And excellent peppermint drops.

Then buy of your Buttercup—dear Little Buttercup;
   Sailors should never be shy;
So, buy of your Buttercup—poor Little Buttercup;
   Come, of your Buttercup buy!

BOAT. Aye, Little Buttercup—and well called—for you're the rosiest, the roundest, and the reddest beauty in all Spithead.

BUT. Red, am I? and round—and rosy! May be, for I have dissembled well! But hark ye, my merry friend—hast ever thought that beneath a gay and frivolous exterior there may lurk a canker-worm which is slowly but surely eating its way into one's very heart?

BOAT. No, my lass, I can't say I've ever thought that.

Enter DICK DEADEYE. *He pushes through sailors, and comes down.*

DICK. *I* have thought it often. (*All recoil from him.*)

BUT. Yes, you look like it! What's the matter with the man? Isn't he well?

BOAT. Don't take no heed of *him;* that's only poor Dick Deadeye.

DICK. I say—it's a beast of a name, ain't it—Dick Deadeye?

BUT. It's not a nice name.

DICK. I'm ugly too, ain't I?

BUT. You are certainly plain.

DICK. And I'm three-cornered too, ain't I?

BUT. You are rather triangular.

DICK. Ha! ha! That's it. I'm ugly, and they hate me for it; for you all hate me, don't you?

ALL. We do!

DICK. There!

BOAT. Well, Dick, we wouldn't go for to hurt any fellow-creature's feelings, but you can't expect a chap with such a name as Dick Deadeye to be a popular character—now can you?

DICK. No.

BOAT. It's asking too much, ain't it?

DICK. It is. From such a face and form as mine the noblest sentiments sound like the black utterances of a depraved imagination. It is human nature—I am resigned.

RECITATIVE

BUT. (*looking down hatchway*).
　　　　But, tell me—who's the youth whose faltering feet
　　　　　　With difficulty bear him on his course?

BOAT. 　　That is the smartest lad in all the fleet—
　　　　　　Ralph Rackstraw!

BUT. 　　Ha! That name! Remorse! remorse!

Enter RALPH *from hatchway.*

MADRIGAL—RALPH

The Nightingale
Sighed for the moon's bright ray,
And told his tale
In his own melodious way!
He sang "Ah, well-a-day!"
ALL. He sang "Ah, well-a-day!"

The lowly vale
For the mountain vainly sighed,
To his humble wail
The echoing hills replied.
They sang "Ah, well-a-day!"
ALL. They sang "Ah, well-a-day!"

RECITATIVE

I know the value of a kindly chorus,
But choruses yield little consolation
When we have pain and sorrow too before us!
I love—and love, alas, above my station!

BUT. (*aside*). He loves—and loves a lass above his station!
ALL (*aside*). Yes, yes, the lass is much above his station!

[*Exit* LITTLE BUTTERCUP.

BALLAD—RALPH

A maiden fair to see,
The pearl of minstrelsy,
  A bud of blushing beauty;
For whom proud nobles sigh,
And with each other vie
  To do her menial's duty.
ALL. To do her menial's duty.

A suitor, lowly born,
With hopeless passion torn,
  And poor beyond denying,
Has dared for her to pine
At whose exalted shrine

A world of wealth is sighing.

ALL.   A world of wealth is sighing.

Unlearned he in aught
Save that which love has taught
    (For love had been his tutor);
Oh, pity, pity me—
Our captain's daughter she,
And I that lowly suitor!

ALL.   And he that lowly suitor!

BOAT. Ah, my poor lad, you've climbed too high: our worthy captain's child won't have nothin' to say to a poor chap like you. Will she, lads?

ALL. No, no!

DICK. No, no, captains' daughters don't marry foremast hands.

ALL. (*recoiling from him*). Shame! shame!

BOAT. Dick Deadeye, them sentiments o' yourn are a disgrace to our common natur'.

RALPH. But it's a strange anomaly, that the daughter of a man who hails from the quarter-deck may not love another who lays out on the fore-yard arm. For a man is but a man, whether he hoists his flag at the main-truck or his slacks on the main-deck.

DICK. Ah, it's a queer world!

RALPH. Dick Deadeye, I have no desire to press hardly on you, but such a revolutionary sentiment is enough to make an honest sailor shudder.

BOAT. My lads, our gallant captain has come on deck; let us greet him as so brave an officer and so gallant a seaman deserves.

Enter CAPTAIN CORCORAN.

RECITATIVE

CAPT. My gallant crew, good morning.

ALL (*saluting*). Sir, good morning!

CAPT. I hope you're all quite well.

ALL (*as before*). Quite well; and you, sir?

CAPT. I am in reasonable health, and happy
      To meet you all once more.
ALL (*as before*). You do us proud, sir!

SONG—CAPT.

CAPT.   I am the Captain of the *Pinafore*;
ALL.   And a right good captain, too!
CAPT.   You're very, very good,
           And be it understood,
        I command a right good crew,
ALL.   We're very, very good,
           And be it understood,
        He commands a right good crew.
CAPT.   Though related to a peer,
        I can hand, reef, and steer,
          And ship a selvagee;
        I am never known to quail
        At the fury of a gale,
          And I'm never, never sick at sea!
ALL.   What, never?
CAPT.   No, never!
ALL.   What, *never*?
CAPT.   Hardly ever!
ALL.   He's hardly ever sick at sea!
        Then give three cheers, and one cheer more,
        For the hardy Captain of the *Pinafore*!

CAPT.	I do my best to satisfy you all—
ALL.	And with you we're quite content.
CAPT.	You're exceedingly polite,
	And I think it only right
	To return the compliment.
ALL.	We're exceedingly polite,
	And he thinks it's only right
	To return the compliment.
CAPT.	Bad language or abuse,
	I never, never use,
	Whatever the emergency;
	Though "Bother it" I may
	Occasionally say,
	I never use a big, big D—
ALL.	What, never?
CAPT.	No, never!
ALL.	What, *never*?
CAPT.	Hardly ever!
ALL.	Hardly ever swears a big, big D—
	Then give three cheers, and one cheer more,
	For the well-bred Captain of the *Pinafore*!

[*After song exeunt all but* CAPTAIN.

Enter LITTLE BUTTERCUP.

RECITATIVE

BUT.	Sir, you are sad! The silent eloquence
	Of yonder tear that trembles on your eyelash
	Proclaims a sorrow far more deep than common;
	Confide in me—fear not—I am a mother!
CAPT.	Yes, Little Buttercup, I'm sad and sorry—
	My daughter, Josephine, the fairest flower
	That ever blossomed on ancestral timber,
	Is sought in marriage by Sir Joseph Porter,
	Our Admiralty's First Lord, but for some reason
	She does not seem to tackle kindly to it.
BUT. (*with emotion*).	Ah, poor Sir Joseph! Ah, I know too well
	The anguish of a heart that loves but vainly!

But see, here comes your most attractive daughter.
I go—Farewell! [*Exit.*

CAPT. (*looking after her*). A plump and pleasing person!
[*Exit.*

Enter JOSEPHINE, *twining some flowers which she carries in a small basket.*

BALLAD—JOSEPHINE

Sorry her lot who loves too well,
  Heavy the heart that hopes but vainly,
Sad are the sighs that own the spell,
  Uttered by eyes that speak too plainly;
  Heavy the sorrow that bows the head
  When love is alive and hope is dead!

Sad is the hour when sets the sun—
  Dark is the night to earth's poor daughters,
When to the ark the wearied one
  Flies from the empty waste of waters!
  Heavy the sorrow that bows the head
  When love is alive and hope is dead!

Enter CAPTAIN.

CAPT. My child, I grieve to see that you are a prey to melancholy.
You should look your best to-day, for Sir Joseph Porter, K.C.B., will be
here this afternoon to claim your promised hand.

JOS. Ah, father, your words cut me to the quick. I can esteem—reverence—venerate Sir Joseph, for he is a great and good man; but oh, I cannot love him! My heart is already given.

CAPT. (*aside*). It is then as I feared. (*Aloud.*) Given? And to whom? Not to some gilded lordling?

JOS. No, father—the object of my love is no lordling. Oh, pity me, for he is but a humble sailor on board your own ship!

CAPT. Impossible!

JOS. Yes, it is true—too true.

CAPT. A common sailor? Oh fie!

JOS. I blush for the weakness that allows me to cherish such a passion. I hate myself when I think of the depth to which I have stooped in permitting myself to think tenderly of one so ignobly born, but I love him! I love him! I love him! (*Weeps.*)

CAPT. Come, my child, let us talk this over. In a matter of the heart I would not coerce my daughter—I attach but little value to rank or wealth, but the line must be drawn somewhere. A man in that station may be brave and worthy, but at every step he would commit solecisms that society would never pardon.

JOS. Oh, I have thought of this night and day. But fear not, father, I have a heart, and therefore I love; but I am your daughter, and therefore I am proud. Though I carry my love with me to the tomb, he shall never, never know it.

CAPT. You *are* my daughter after all. But see, Sir Joseph's barge approaches, manned by twelve trusty oarsmen and accompanied by the admiring crowd of sisters, cousins, and aunts that attend him wherever he goes. Retire, my daughter, to your cabin—take this, his photograph, with you—it may help to bring you to a more reasonable frame of mind.

JOS. My own thoughtful father!

[*Exit* JOSEPHINE. CAPTAIN *remains and ascends the poop-deck.*

BARCAROLLE (*invisible*)

Over the bright blue sea
Comes Sir Joseph Porter, K.C.B.,
Wherever he may go
Bang-bang the loud nine-pounders go!

W. S. GILBERT

Shout o'er the bright blue sea
For Sir Joseph Porter, K.C.B.

(During this the Crew have entered on tiptoe, listening attentively to the song.)

CHORUS OF SAILORS

Sir Joseph's barge is seen,
    And its crowd of blushing beauties,
We hope he'll find us clean,
    And attentive to our duties.
We sail, we sail the ocean blue,
    And our saucy ship's a beauty.
We're sober, sober men and true
    And attentive to our duty.
We're smart and sober men,
    And quite devoid of fe-ar,
In all the Royal N.
    None are so smart as we are.

Enter SIR JOSEPH'S FEMALE RELATIVES.

They dance round stage

REL.   Gaily tripping,
                    Lightly skipping,
              Flock the maidens to the shipping.
SAILORS.   Flags and guns and pennants dipping!
              All the ladies love the shipping.

REL.   Sailors sprightly
                Always rightly
                Welcome ladies so politely.

SAILORS.   Ladies who can smile so brightly,
                Sailors welcome most politely.

CAPT. (*from poop*). Now give three cheers, I'll lead the way.

ALL.   Hurrah! hurrah! hurrah! hurray!

Enter SIR JOSEPH *with* COUSIN HEBE.

SONG—SIR JOSEPH

I am the monarch of the sea,
    The ruler of the Queen's Navee,
Whose praise Great Britain loudly chants.

COUSIN HEBE. And we are his sisters, and his cousins, and his aunts!

REL.   And we are his sisters, and his cousins, and his aunts!

SIR JOSEPH.   When at anchor here I ride,
              My bosom swells with pride,
           And I snap my fingers at a foeman's taunts;

COUSIN HEBE. And so do his sisters, and his cousins, and his aunts!

ALL.   And so do his sisters, and his cousins, and his aunts!

SIR JOSEPH.   But when the breezes blow,
             I generally go below,
           And seek the seclusion that a cabin grants!

COUSIN HEBE. And so do his sisters, and his cousins, and his aunts!

ALL.   And so do his sisters, and his cousins, and his aunts!
          His sisters and his cousins,
          Whom he reckons up by dozens,
            And his aunts!

SONG—SIR JOSEPH

When I was a lad I served a term
As office boy to an Attorney's firm.
I cleaned the windows and I swept the floor,
And I polished up the handle of the big front door.
    I polished up that handle so carefullee
    That now I am the Ruler of the Queen's Navee!

CHORUS.—He polished, etc.

25

As office boy I made such a mark
That they gave me the post of a junior clerk.
I served the writs with a smile so bland,
And I copied all the letters in a big round hand—
    I copied all the letters in a hand so free,
    That now I am the Ruler of the Queen's Navee!

    CHORUS.—He copied, etc.

In serving writs I made such a name
That an articled clerk I soon became;
I wore clean collars and a brand-new suit
For the pass examination at the Institute.
    And that pass examination did so well for me,
    That now I am the Ruler of the Queen's Navee!

    CHORUS.—And that pass examination, etc.

Of legal knowledge I acquired such a grip
That they took me into the partnership.
And that junior partnership, I ween,
Was the only ship that I ever had seen.
    But that kind of ship so suited me,
    That now I am the Ruler of the Queen's Navee!

    CHORUS.—But that kind, etc.

I grew so rich that I was sent
By a pocket borough into Parliament.
I always voted at my party's call,
And I never thought of thinking for myself at all.
    I thought so little, they rewarded me
    By making me the Ruler of the Queen's Navee!

    CHORUS.—He thought so little, etc.

Now landsmen all, whoever you may be,
If you want to rise to the top of the tree,
If your soul isn't fettered to an office stool,
Be careful to be guided by this golden rule—
    Stick close to your desks and never go to sea,
    And you all may be Rulers of the Queen's Navee!

    CHORUS.—Stick close, etc.

SIR JOSEPH. You've a remarkably fine crew, Captain Corcoran.

CAPT. It *is* a fine crew, Sir Joseph.

SIR JOSEPH (*examining a very small midshipman*). A British sailor is a splendid fellow, Captain Corcoran.

CAPT. A splendid fellow indeed, Sir Joseph.

SIR JOSEPH. I hope you treat your crew kindly, Captain Corcoran.

CAPT. Indeed I hope so, Sir Joseph.

SIR JOSEPH. Never forget that they are the bulwarks of England's greatness, Captain Corcoran.

CAPT. So I have always considered them, Sir Joseph.

SIR JOSEPH. No bullying, I trust—no strong language of any kind, eh?

CAPT. Oh, never, Sir Joseph.

SIR JOSEPH. What, *never*?

CAPT. Hardly ever, Sir Joseph. They are an excellent crew, and do their work thoroughly without it.

SIR JOSEPH. Don't patronise them, sir—pray, don't patronise them.

CAPT. Certainly not, Sir Joseph.

SIR JOSEPH. That you are their captain is an accident of birth. I cannot permit these noble fellows to be patronised because an accident of birth has placed you above them and them below you.

CAPT. I am the last person to insult a British sailor, Sir Joseph.

SIR JOSEPH. You are the last person who did, Captain Corcoran. Desire that splendid seaman to step forward.

(DICK *comes forward.*)

SIR JOSEPH. No, no, the other splendid seaman.

CAPT. Ralph Rackstraw, three paces to the front—march!

SIR JOSEPH (*sternly*). If what?

CAPT. I beg your pardon—I don't think I understand you.

SIR JOSEPH. If you *please.*

CAPT. Oh, yes, of course. If you please. (RALPH *steps forward.*)

SIR JOSEPH. You're a remarkably fine fellow.

RALPH. Yes, your honour.

SIR JOSEPH. And a first-rate seaman, I'll be bound.

RALPH. There's not a smarter topman in the Navy, your honour, though I say it who shouldn't.

SIR JOSEPH. Not at all. Proper self-respect, nothing more. Can you dance a hornpipe?

RALPH. No, your honour.

SIR JOSEPH. That's a pity: all sailors should dance hornpipes. I will teach you one this evening, after dinner. Now tell me—don't be afraid—how does your captain treat you, eh?

RALPH. A better captain don't walk the deck, your honour.

ALL. Aye! Aye!

SIR JOSEPH. Good. I like to hear you speak well of your commanding officer; I daresay he don't deserve it, but still it does you credit. Can you sing?

RALPH. I can hum a little, your honour.

SIR JOSEPH. Then hum this at your leisure. (*Giving him MS. music.*) It is a song that I have composed for the use of the Royal Navy. It is designed to encourage independence of thought and action in the lower branches of the service, and to teach the principle that a British sailor is any man's equal, excepting mine. Now, Captain Corcoran, a word with you in your cabin, on a tender and sentimental subject.

CAPT. Aye, aye, Sir Joseph. (*Crossing.*) Boatswain, in commemoration of this joyous occasion, see that extra grog is served out to the ship's company at seven bells.

BOAT. Beg pardon. If what, your honour?

CAPT. If what? I don't think I understand you.

BOAT. If you *please*, your honour.

CAPT. What!

SIR JOSEPH. The gentleman is quite right. If you *please*.

CAPT. (*stamping his foot impatiently*). If you *please*!

[*Exit.*

SIR JOSEPH.   For I hold that on the seas
        The expression, "if you please",
           A particularly gentlemanly tone implants.

COUSIN HEBE. And so do his sisters, and his cousins, and his aunts!

ALL.   And so do his sisters, and his cousins, and his aunts!

[*Exeunt* SIR JOSEPH *and* RELATIVES.

BOAT. Ah! Sir Joseph's a true gentleman; courteous and considerate to the very humblest.

RALPH. True, Boatswain, but we are not the very humblest. Sir Joseph has explained our true position to us. As he says, a British seaman is any man's equal excepting his, and if Sir Joseph says that, is it not our duty to believe him?

ALL. Well spoke! well spoke!

DICK. You're on a wrong tack, and so is he. He means well, but he don't know. When people have to obey other people's orders, equality's out of the question.

ALL (*recoiling*). Horrible! horrible!

BOAT. Dick Deadeye, if you go for to infuriate this here ship's company too far, I won't answer for being able to hold 'em in. I'm shocked! that's what I am—shocked.

RALPH. Messmates, my mind's made up. I'll speak to the captain's daughter, and tell her, like an honest man, of the honest love I have for her.

ALL. Aye, aye!

RALPH. Is not my love as good as another's? Is not my heart as true as another's? Have I not hands and eyes and ears and limbs like another?

ALL. Aye, aye!

RALPH. True, I lack birth——

29

BOAT. You've a berth on board this very ship.

RALPH. Well said—I had forgotten that. Messmates—what do you say? Do you approve my determination?

ALL. We do.

DICK. *I* don't.

BOAT. What is to be done with this here hopeless chap? Let us sing him the song that Sir Joseph has kindly composed for us. Perhaps it will bring this here miserable creetur to a proper state of mind.

GLEE—RALPH, BOATSWAIN, BOATSWAIN'S MATE, *and* CHORUS

A British tar is a soaring soul,
    As free as a mountain bird,
His energetic fist should be ready to resist
    A dictatorial word.
His nose should pant and his lip should curl,
His cheeks should flame and his brow should furl,
His bosom should heave and his heart should glow,
And his fist be ever ready for a knock-down blow.

CHORUS.—His nose should pant, etc.

His eyes should flash with an inborn fire,
    His brow with scorn be wrung;
He never should bow down to a domineering frown,
    Or the tang of a tyrant tongue.

30

His foot should stamp and his throat should growl,
His hair should twirl and his face should scowl;
His eyes should flash and his breast protrude,
And this should be his customary attitude—(*pose*).

CHORUS.—His foot should stamp, etc.

(*All dance off excepting* RALPH, *who remains, leaning pensively against bulwark.*)

Enter JOSEPHINE *from cabin.*

JOS. It is useless—Sir Joseph's attentions nauseate me. I know that he is a truly great and good man, for he told me so himself, but to me he seems tedious, fretful, and dictatorial. Yet his must be a mind of no common order, or he would not dare to teach my dear father to dance a hornpipe on the cabin table. (*Sees* RALPH.) Ralph Rackstraw! (*Overcome by emotion.*)

RALPH. Aye, lady—no other than poor Ralph Rackstraw!

JOS. (*aside*). How my heart beats! (*Aloud.*) And why poor, Ralph?

RALPH. I am poor in the essence of happiness, lady—rich only in never-ending unrest. In me there meet a combination of antithetical elements which are at eternal war with one another. Driven hither by objective influences—thither by subjective emotions—wafted one moment into blazing day, by mocking hope—plunged the next into the Cimmerian darkness of tangible despair, I am but a living ganglion of irreconcilable antagonisms. I hope I make myself clear, lady?

JOS. Perfectly. (*Aside.*) His simple eloquence goes to my heart. Oh, if I dared—but no, the thought is madness! (*Aloud.*) Dismiss these foolish fancies, they torture you but needlessly. Come, make one effort.

RALPH (*aside*). I will—one. (*Aloud.*) Josephine!

JOS. (*indignantly*). Sir!

RALPH. Aye, even though Jove's armoury were launched at the head of the audacious mortal whose lips, unhallowed by relationship, dared to breathe that precious word, yet would I breathe it once, and then perchance be silent evermore. Josephine, in one brief breath I will concentrate the hopes, the doubts, the anxious fears of six weary months. Josephine, I am a British sailor, and I love you!

JOS. Sir, this audacity! (*Aside.*) Oh, my heart, my beating heart!

(*Aloud.*) This unwarrantable presumption on the part of a common sailor! (*Aside.*) Common! oh, the irony of the word! (*Crossing, aloud.*) Oh, sir, you forget the disparity in our ranks.

RALPH. I forget nothing, haughty lady. I love you desperately, my life is in your hand—I lay it at your feet! Give me hope, and what I lack in education and polite accomplishments, that I will endeavour to acquire. Drive me to despair, and in death alone I shall look for consolation. I am proud and cannot stoop to implore. I have spoken and I wait your word.

JOS. You shall not wait long. Your proffered love I haughtily reject. Go, sir, and learn to cast your eyes on some village maiden in your own poor rank—they should be lowered before your captain's daughter!

DUET—JOSEPHINE *and* RALPH

JOS.
Refrain, audacious tar,
  Your suit from pressing,
Remember what you are,
  And whom addressing!

(*Aside.*)
I'd laugh my rank to scorn
  In union holy,
Were he more highly born
  Or I more lowly!

RALPH.
Proud lady, have your way,
  Unfeeling beauty!
You speak and I obey,
  It is my duty!
I am the lowliest tar
  That sails the water,
And you, proud maiden, are
  My captain's daughter!

(*Aside.*)
My heart with anguish torn
  Bows down before her,
She laughs my love to scorn,
  Yet I adore her!

[*Repeat refrain, ensemble, then exit* JOSEPHINE *into cabin.*

RALPH (*Recit.*).
Can I survive this overbearing
Or live a life of mad despairing,

32

My proffered love despised, rejected?
No, no, it's not to be expected!
(*Calling off.*)
Messmates, ahoy!
Come here! Come here!

Enter SAILORS, HEBE, *and* RELATIVES.

ALL.   Aye, aye, my boy,
     What cheer, what cheer?
      Now tell us, pray,
      Without delay,
      What does she say—
     What cheer, what cheer?

RALPH (*to* COUSIN HEBE).
    The maiden treats my suit with scorn,
     Rejects my humble gift, my lady;
    She says I am ignobly born,
     And cuts my hopes adrift, my lady.

ALL.   Oh, cruel one.

DICK.   She spurns your suit? Oho! Oho!
    I told you so, I told you so.

SAILORS *and* RELATIVES.

  Shall $\begin{Bmatrix} we \\ they \end{Bmatrix}$ submit? Are $\begin{Bmatrix} we \\ they \end{Bmatrix}$ but slaves?
    Love comes alike to high and low—
    Britannia's sailors rule the waves,
     And shall they stoop to insult? No!

DICK.   You must submit, you are but slaves;
     A lady she! Oho! Oho!
    You lowly toilers of the waves,
     She spurns you all—I told you so!

RALPH.   My friends, my leave of life I'm taking,
    For oh, my heart, my heart is breaking.
    When I am gone, oh, prithee tell
    The maid that, as I died, I loved her well!

ALL (*turning away, weeping*).
    Of life, alas! his leave he's taking,
    For ah! his faithful heart is breaking;

When he is gone we'll surely tell
The maid that, as he died, he loved her well.

(*During Chorus* BOATSWAIN *has loaded pistol, which he hands to* RALPH.)

RALPH.   Be warned, my messmates all
      Who love in rank above you—
     For Josephine I fall!

(*Puts pistol to his head. All the sailors stop their ears.*)

Enter JOSEPHINE *on deck.*

JOS.   Ah! stay your hand! I love you!
ALL.   Ah! stay your hand—she loves you!
RALPH (*incredulously*). Loves me?
JOS.   Loves you!
ALL.   Yes, yes—ah, yes,—she loves you!

ENSEMBLE

SAILORS *and* RELATIVES *and* JOSEPHINE

Oh joy, oh rapture unforeseen,
For now the sky is all serene;
The god of day—the orb of love—
Has hung his ensign high above,
  The sky is all ablaze.
With wooing words and loving song,
We'll chase the lagging hours along,

And if $\left\{\begin{array}{l} \text{I find} \\ \text{we find} \end{array}\right\}$ the maiden coy,

$\left.\begin{array}{l} \text{We'll} \\ \text{I'll} \end{array}\right\}$ murmur forth decorous joy

  In dreamy roundelays!

DICK DEADEYE

He thinks he's won his Josephine,
But though the sky is now serene,
A frowning thunderbolt above
May end their ill-assorted love
  Which now is all ablaze.

34

Our captain, ere the day is gone,
Will be extremely down upon
The wicked men who art employ
To make his Josephine less coy
In many various ways.   [*Exit* DICK.

JOS.	This very night,
HEBE.	With bated breath
RALPH.	And muffled oar—
JOS.	Without a light,
HEBE.	As still as death,
RALPH.	We'll steal ashore.
JOS.	A clergyman
RALPH.	Shall make us one
BOAT.	At half-past ten,
JOS.	And then we can
RALPH.	Return, for none
BOAT.	Can part them then!
ALL.	This very night, etc

(DICK *appears at hatchway*.)

DICK.   Forbear, nor carry out the scheme you've planned;
She is a lady—you a foremast hand!
Remember, she's your gallant captain's daughter,
And you the meanest slave that crawls the water!

ALL.   Back, vermin, back,
              Nor mock us!
           Back, vermin, back,
              You shock us!

[*Exit* DICK.

Let's give three cheers for the sailor's bride
Who casts all thought of rank aside—
Who gives up home and fortune too
For the honest love of a sailor true!
  For a British tar is a soaring soul
    As free as a mountain bird!
  His energetic fist should be ready to resist
    A dictatorial word!

His foot should stamp and his throat should growl,
His hair should twirl and his face should scowl,
His eyes should flash and his breast protrude,
And this should be his customary attitude—(*pose*).

GENERAL DANCE

END OF ACT I

ACT TWO

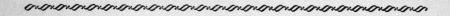

Same Scene. *Night. Awning removed. Moonlight.*

CAPTAIN *discovered singing on poop-deck, and accompanying himself on a mandolin.* LITTLE BUTTERCUP *seated on quarter-deck, gazing sentimentally at him.*

SONG—CAPTAIN

Fair moon, to thee I sing
    Bright regent of the heavens,
Say, why is everything
    Either at sixes or at sevens?
I have lived hitherto
    Free from breath of slander,
Beloved by all my crew—
    A really popular commander.
But now my kindly crew rebel,
    My daughter to a tar is partial,
Sir Joseph storms, and, sad to tell,
    He threatens a court martial!
    Fair moon, to thee I sing,
        Bright regent of the heavens,
    Say, why is everything
        Either at sixes or at sevens?

BUT. How sweetly he carols forth his melody to the unconscious moon! Of whom is he thinking? Of some high-born beauty? It may

37

be! Who is poor Little Buttercup that she should expect his glance to fall on one so lowly! And yet if he knew—if he only knew!

CAPT. (*coming down*). Ah! Little Buttercup, still on board? That is not quite right, little one. It would have been more respectable to have gone on shore at dusk.

BUT. True, dear Captain—but the recollection of your sad pale face seemed to chain me to the ship. I would fain see you smile before I go.

CAPT. Ah! Little Buttercup, I fear it will be long before I recover my accustomed cheerfulness, for misfortunes crowd upon me, and all my old friends seem to have turned against me!

BUT. Oh no—do not say "all", dear Captain. That were unjust to one, at least.

CAPT. True, for you are staunch to me. (*Aside.*) If ever I gave my heart again, methinks it would be to such a one as this! (*Aloud.*) I am touched to the heart by your innocent regard for me, and were we differently situated, I think I could have returned it. But as it is, I fear I can never be more to you than a friend.

BUT. I understand! You hold aloof from me because you are rich and lofty—and I poor and lowly. But take care! The poor bumboat woman has gipsy blood in her veins, and she can read destinies.

CAPT. Destinies?

BUT. There is a change in store for you!

CAPT. A change?

BUT. Aye—be prepared!

DUET.—LITTLE BUTTERCUP *and* CAPTAIN

BUT.   Things are seldom what they seem,
          Skim milk masquerades as cream;
          Highlows pass as patent leathers;
          Jackdaws strut in peacock's feathers.

CAPT. (*puzzled*).   Very true,
          So they do.

BUT.   Black sheep dwell in every fold;
          All that glitters is not gold;
          Storks turn out to be but logs;
          Bulls are but inflated frogs.

CAPT. (*puzzled*).　　So they be,
　　　　　　　　　　Frequentlee.

BUT.　　Drops the wind and stops the mill;
　　　　Turbot is ambitious brill;
　　　　Gild the farthing if you will,
　　　　Yet it is a farthing still.

CAPT. (*puzzled*).　　Yes, I know,
　　　　　　　　　　That is so.
　　Though to catch your drift I'm striving,
　　　　It is shady—it is shady;
　　I don't see at what you're driving,
　　　　Mystic lady—mystic lady,

(*Aside.*)　　Stern conviction's o'er me stealing,
　　　　　　That the mystic lady's dealing
　　　　　　In oracular revealing.

BUT. (*aside*).　　Stern conviction's o'er him stealing,
　　　　　　　　That the mystic lady's dealing
　　　　　　　　In oracular revealing.

BOTH.　　Yes, I know—
　　　　　That is so!

CAPT.　　Though I'm anything but clever,
　　　　I could talk like that for ever:
　　　　Once a cat was killed by care;
　　　　Only brave deserve the fair.

BUT.	Very true, So they do.
CAPT.	Wink is often good as nod; Spoils the child who spares the rod; Thirsty lambs run foxy dangers; Dogs are found in many mangers.
BUT.	Frequentlee, I agree.
CAPT.	Paw of cat the chestnut snatches; Worn-out garments show new patches; Only count the chick that hatches; Men are grown-up catchy-catchies.
BUT.	Yes, I know, That is so.
(*Aside.*)	Though to catch my drift he's striving, I'll dissemble—I'll dissemble; When he sees at what I'm driving, Let him tremble—let him tremble!

ENSEMBLE

Though a mystic tone $\left\{\begin{array}{c}\text{I}\\\text{you}\end{array}\right\}$ borrow,

$\left.\begin{array}{l}\text{You will}\\\text{I shall}\end{array}\right\}$ learn the truth with sorrow,

Here to-day and gone to-morrow;
Yes, I know—
That is so!

[*At the end exit* LITTLE BUTTERCUP *melodramatically.*

CAPT. Incomprehensible as her utterances are, I nevertheless feel that they are dictated by a sincere regard for me. But to what new misery is she referring? Time alone can tell!

Enter SIR JOSEPH.

SIR JOSEPH. Captain Corcoran, I am much disappointed with your daughter. In fact, I don't think she will do.

CAPT. She won't do, Sir Joseph!

SIR JOSEPH. I'm afraid not. The fact is, that although I have urged my suit with as much eloquence as is consistent with an official utterance, I have done so hitherto without success. How do you account for this?

CAPT. Really, Sir Joseph, I hardly know. Josephine is of course sensible of your condescension.

SIR JOSEPH. She naturally would be.

CAPT. But perhaps your exalted rank dazzles her.

SIR JOSEPH. You think it does?

CAPT. I can hardly say; but she is a modest girl, and her social position is far below your own. It may be that she feels she is not worthy of you.

SIR JOSEPH. That is really a very sensible suggestion, and displays more knowledge of human nature than I had given you credit for.

CAPT. See, she comes. If your lordship would kindly reason with her and assure her officially that it is a standing rule at the Admiralty that love levels all ranks, her respect for an official utterance might induce her to look upon your offer in its proper light.

SIR JOSEPH. It is not unlikely. I will adopt your suggestion. But soft, she is here. Let us withdraw, and watch our opportunity.

Enter JOSEPHINE *from cabin.* FIRST LORD *and* CAPTAIN *retire.*

SCENA—JOSEPHINE

The hours creep on apace,
   My guilty heart is quaking!
Oh, that I might retrace
   The step that I am taking!
Its folly it were easy to be showing,
What I am giving up and whither going.
On the one hand, papa's luxurious home,
   Hung with ancestral armour and old brasses,
Carved oak and tapestry from distant Rome,
   Rare "blue and white" Venetian finger-glasses,
Rich oriental rugs, luxurious sofa pillows,
And everything that isn't old, from Gillow's.

And on the other, a dark and dingy room,
  In some back street with stuffy children crying,
Where organs yell, and clacking housewives fume,
  And clothes are hanging out all day a-drying.
With one cracked looking-glass to see your face in,
And dinner served up in a pudding basin!

  A simple sailor, lowly born,
    Unlettered and unknown,
  Who toils for bread from early morn
    Till half the night has flown!
  No golden rank can he impart—
    No wealth of house or land—
  No fortune save his trusty heart
    And honest brown right hand!
  And yet he is so wondrous fair
  That love for one so passing rare,
  So peerless in his manly beauty,
  Were little else than solemn duty!
Oh, god of love, and god of reason, say,
Which of you twain shall my poor heart obey!

SIR JOSEPH and CAPTAIN enter.

SIR JOSEPH. Madam, it has been represented to me that you are appalled by my exalted rank. I desire to convey to you officially my assurance, that if your hesitation is attributable to that circumstance, it is uncalled for.

JOS. Oh! then your lordship is of opinion that married happiness is *not* inconsistent with discrepancy in rank?

SIR JOSEPH. I am officially of that opinion.

JOS. That the high and the lowly may be truly happy together, provided that they truly love one another?

SIR JOSEPH. Madam, I desire to convey to you officially my opinion that love is a platform upon which all ranks meet.

JOS. I thank you, Sir Joseph. I *did* hesitate, but I will hesitate no longer. (*Aside.*) He little thinks how eloquently he has pleaded his rival's cause!

42

TRIO

FIRST LORD, CAPTAIN, *and* JOSEPHINE

CAPT.	Never mind the why and wherefore,
	Love can level ranks, and therefore,
	Though his lordship's station's mighty,
	Though stupendous be his brain,
	Though your tastes are mean and flighty
	And your fortune poor and plain,
CAPT. *and*	Ring the merry bells on board-ship,
SIR JOSEPH.	Rend the air with warbling wild,

For the union of $\begin{Bmatrix} \text{his} \\ \text{my} \end{Bmatrix}$ lordship

With a humble captain's child!

CAPT.	For a humble captain's daughter—
JOS.	For a gallant captain's daughter—
SIR JOSEPH.	And a lord who rules the water—
JOS. (*aside*).	And a *tar* who ploughs the water!
ALL.	Let the air with joy be laden,
	Rend with songs the air above,
	For the union of a maiden
	With the man who owns her love!
SIR JOSEPH.	Never mind the why and wherefore,
	Love can level ranks, and therefore,
	Though your nautical relation (*alluding to* CAPT.)
	In my set could scarcely pass—
	Though you occupy a station
	In the lower middle class—
CAPT. *and*	Ring the merry bells on board-ship,
SIR JOSEPH.	Rend the air with warbling wild,

For the union of $\begin{Bmatrix} \text{my} \\ \text{his} \end{Bmatrix}$ lordship

With a humble captain's child!

CAPT.	For a humble captain's daughter—
JOS.	For a gallant captain's daughter—
SIR JOSEPH.	And a lord who rules the water—
JOS. (*aside*).	And a *tar* who ploughs the water!
ALL.	Let the air with joy be laden,
	Rend with songs the air above,

> For the union of a maiden
>> With the man who owns her love!

JOS.   Never mind the why and wherefore,
> Love can level ranks, and therefore,
> I admit the jurisdiction;
>> Ably have you played your part;
> You have carried firm conviction
>> To my hesitating heart.

CAPT. *and*
SIR JOSEPH.   Ring the merry bells on board-ship,
> Rend the air with warbling wild,

For the union of $\left\{\begin{matrix} my \\ his \end{matrix}\right\}$ lordship

> With a humble captain's child!

CAPT.   For a humble captain's daughter—

JOS.   For a gallant captain's daughter—

SIR JOSEPH.   And a lord who rules the water—

JOS. (*aside*).   And a *tar* who ploughs the water!

(*Aloud.*)   Let the air with joy be laden.

CAPT. *and* SIR JOSEPH.   Ring the merry bells on board-ship—

JOS.   For the union of a maiden—

CAPT. *and* SIR JOSEPH.   For her union with his lordship.

ALL.   Rend with songs the air above
> For the man who owns her love!

[*Exit* JOS.

CAPT. Sir Joseph, I cannot express to you my delight at the happy result of your eloquence. Your argument was unanswerable.

SIR JOSEPH. Captain Corcoran, it is one of the happiest characteristics of this glorious country that official utterances are invariably regarded as unanswerable.

[*Exit* SIR JOSEPH.

CAPT. At last my fond hopes are to be crowned. My only daughter is to be the bride of a Cabinet Minister. The prospect is Elysian. (*During this speech* DICK DEADEYE *has entered.*)

DICK. Captain.

CAPT. Deadeye! You here? Don't! (*Recoiling from him.*)

DICK. Ah, don't shrink from me, Captain. I'm unpleasant to look at, and my name's agin me, but I ain't as bad as I seem.

CAPT. What would you with me?

DICK (*mysteriously*). I'm come to give you warning.

CAPT. Indeed! do you propose to leave the Navy then?

DICK. No, no, you misunderstand me; listen!

DUET

CAPTAIN *and* DICK DEADEYE

DICK.   Kind Captain, I've important information,
　　　　Sing hey, the kind commander that you are,
　　About a certain intimate relation,
　　　　Sing hey, the merry maiden and the tar.

BOTH.　　　　The merry maiden and the tar.

CAPT.   Good fellow, in conundrums you are speaking,
　　　　Sing hey, the mystic sailor that you are;
　　The answer to them vainly I am seeking;
　　　　Sing hey, the merry maiden and the tar.

BOTH.　　　　The merry maiden and the tar.

DICK.   Kind Captain, your young lady is a-sighing,
　　　　Sing hey, the simple captain that you are,
　　This very night with Rackstraw to be flying;
　　　　Sing hey, the merry maiden and the tar.

BOTH.　　　　The merry maiden and the tar.

45

CAPT.   Good fellow, you have given timely warning,
      Sing hey, the thoughtful sailor that you are,
    I'll talk to Master Rackstraw in the morning:
      Sing hey, the cat-o'-nine-tails and the tar.

                        (Producing a "cat".)

BOTH.   The merry cat-o'-nine-tails and the tar!

CAPT. Dick Deadeye—I thank you for your warning—I will at once take means to arrest their flight. This boat cloak will afford me ample disguise—So! (*Envelops himself in a mysterious cloak, holding it before his face.*)

DICK. Ha, ha! They are foiled—foiled—foiled!

Enter Crew on tiptoe, with RALPH *and* BOATSWAIN *meeting* JOSEPHINE, *who enters from cabin on tiptoe, with bundle of necessaries, and accompanied by* LITTLE BUTTERCUP.

ENSEMBLE

Carefully on tiptoe stealing,
    Breathing gently as we may,
Every step with caution feeling,
    We will softly steal away.
      (CAPTAIN *stamps.*)--*Chord*

ALL (*much alarmed*).   Goodness me—
      Why, what was that?

DICK.   Silent be,
      It was the cat!

ALL (*reassured*).   It was—it was the cat!

CAPT. (*producing cat-o'-nine-tails*). They're right, it was the cat!

ALL.   Pull ashore, in fashion steady,
      Hymen will defray the fare,
For a clergyman is ready
    To unite the happy pair!
      (*Stamp as before, and Chord.*)

ALL.   Goodness me,
      Why, what was that?

DICK.   Silent be,
      Again the cat!

ALL. It was again that cat!

CAPT. (*aside*). They're right, it was the cat!

CAPT. (*throwing off cloak*). Hold! (*All start.*)

Pretty daughter of mine,
I insist upon knowing
Where you may be going
With these sons of the brine,
For my excellent crew,
Though foes they could thump any,
Are scarcely fit company,
My daughter, for you.

CREW. Now, hark at that, do!

Though foes we could thump any,
We are scarcely fit company
For a lady like you!

RALPH. Proud officer, that haughty lip uncurl!

Vain man, suppress that supercilious sneer,
For I have dared to love your matchless girl,
A fact well known to all my messmates here!

CAPT. Oh, horror!

RALPH *and* JOS. $\begin{Bmatrix} \text{I,} \\ \text{He,} \end{Bmatrix}$ humble, poor, and lowly born,

The meanest in the port division—
The butt of epauletted scorn—
The mark of quarter-deck derision—
$\begin{Bmatrix} \text{Have} \\ \text{Has} \end{Bmatrix}$ dared to raise $\begin{Bmatrix} \text{my} \\ \text{his} \end{Bmatrix}$ wormy eyes

Above the dust to which you'd mould $\begin{Bmatrix} \text{me} \\ \text{him} \end{Bmatrix}$

In manhood's glorious pride to rise,
$\begin{Bmatrix} \text{I am} \\ \text{He is} \end{Bmatrix}$ an Englishman—behold $\begin{Bmatrix} \text{me!} \\ \text{him!} \end{Bmatrix}$

ALL. He is an Englishman!

BOAT. He is an Englishman!

For he himself has said it,
And it's greatly to his credit,
That he is an Englishman!

ALL. That he is an Englishman!

BOAT.	For he might have been a Roosian,
	A French, or Turk, or Proosian,
	Or perhaps Itali-an!
ALL.	Or perhaps Itali-an!
BOAT.	But in spite of all temptations
	To belong to other nations,
	He remains an Englishman!
ALL.	For in spite of all temptations, etc.

CAPT. (*trying to repress his anger*).

In uttering a reprobation
  To any British tar,
I try to speak with moderation,
  But you have gone too far.
I'm very sorry to disparage
  A humble foremast lad,
But to seek your captain's child in marriage,
  Why, damme, it's too bad!

During this, COUSIN HEBE *and* FEMALE RELATIVES *have entered.*

ALL (*shocked*).	Oh!
CAPT.	Yes, damme, it's too bad!
ALL.	Oh!
CAPT. *and* DICK DEADEYE.	Yes, damme, it's too bad

During this, SIR JOSEPH *has appeared on poop-deck. He is horrified at the bad language.*

HEBE.   Did you hear him—did you hear him?
    Oh, the monster overbearing!
Don't go near him—don't go near him—
    He is swearing—he is swearing!

SIR JOSEPH. My pain and my distress,
    I find it is not easy to express;
My amazement—my surprise—
    You may learn from the expression of my eyes!

CAPT.   My lord—one word—the facts are not before you
The word was injudicious, I allow—
But hear my explanation, I implore you,
And you will be indignant too, I vow!

SIR JOSEPH.   I will hear of no defence,
      Attempt none if you're sensible.
That word of evil sense
    Is wholly indefensible
Go, ribald, get you hence
    To your cabin with celerity.
This is the consequence
    Of ill-advised asperity!

[*Exit* CAPTAIN, *disgraced, followed by* JOSEPHINE.

ALL.   This is the consequence,
    Of ill-advised asperity!

SIR JOSEPH.   For I'll teach you all, ere long,
      To refrain from language strong.
For I haven't any sympathy for ill-bred taunts!

HEBE.   No more have his sisters, nor his cousins, nor his aunts.

ALL.   For he is an Englishman, etc.

SIR JOSEPH. Now, tell me, my fine fellow—for you *are* a fine fellow——

RALPH. Yes, your honour.

SIR JOSEPH. How came your captain so far to forget himself? I am quite sure you had given him no cause for annoyance.

RALPH. Please your honour, it was thus-wise. You see I'm only a topman—a mere foremast hand——

SIR JOSEPH. Don't be ashamed of that. Your position as a topman is a very exalted one.

RALPH. Well, your honour, love burns as brightly in the fo'c'sle as it does on the quarter-deck, and Josephine is the fairest bud that ever blossomed upon the tree of a poor fellow's wildest hopes.

Enter JOSEPHINE; *she rushes to* RALPH's *arms.*

JOS. Darling! (SIR JOSEPH *horrified.*)

RALPH. She is the figurehead of my ship of life—the bright beacon that guides me into my port of happiness—the rarest, the purest gem that ever sparkled on a poor but worthy fellow's trusting brow!

ALL. Very pretty, very pretty!

SIR JOSEPH. Insolent sailor, you shall repent this outrage. Seize him! (*Two Marines seize him and handcuff him.*)

JOS. Oh, Sir Joseph, spare him, for I love him tenderly.

SIR JOSEPH. Pray, don't. I will teach this presumptuous mariner to discipline his affections. Have you such a thing as a dungeon on board?

ALL. We have!

DICK. They have!

SIR JOSEPH. Then load him with chains and take him there at once!

OCTETTE

RALPH.

> Farewell, my own,
>> Light of my life, farewell!
> For crime unknown
>> I go to a dungeon cell.

JOS.

> I will atone.
>> In the meantime farewell!
> And all alone
>> Rejoice in your dungeon cell!

SIR JOSEPH.

> A bone, a bone
>> I'll pick with this sailor fell;
> Let him be shown
>> At once to his dungeon cell.

BOATSWAIN, DICK DEADEYE, *and* COUSIN HEBE

He'll hear no tone
 Of the maiden he loves so well!
No telephone
 Communicates with his cell!

BUT. (*mysteriously*). But when is known
  The secret I have to tell,
 Wide will be thrown
  The door of his dungeon cell.

ALL.   For crime unknown
      He goes to a dungeon cell!

        [RALPH *is led off in custody.*

SIR JOSEPH. My pain and my distress
     Again it is not easy to express.
     My amazement, my surprise,
     Again you may discover from my eyes.
ALL.   How terrible the aspect of his eyes!
BUT.   Hold! Ere upon your loss
      You lay much stress,
     A long-concealèd crime
      I would confess.

SONG—BUTTERCUP

  A many years ago,
When I was young and charming,
  As some of you may know,
I practised baby-farming.
ALL.   Now this is most alarming!
     When she was young and charming
     She practised baby-farming,
      A many years ago.
BUT.   Two tender babes I nussed:
      One was of low condition.
     The other, upper crust,
      A regular patrician.

ALL (*explaining to each other*).

Now, this is the position:
One was of low condition
The other a patrician,
  A many years ago.

BUT.

Oh, bitter is my cup!
  However could I do it?
I mixed those children up,
  And not a creature knew it!

ALL.

However could you do it?
Some day, no doubt, you'll rue it,
Although no creature knew it,
  So many years ago.

BUT.

In time each little waif
  Forsook his foster-mother
The well-born babe was Ralph—
  Your captain was the other! ! !

ALL.

They left their foster-mother,
The one was Ralph, our brother,
Our captain was the other,
  A many years ago.

SIR JOSEPH. Then I am to understand that Captain Corcoran and Ralph were exchanged in childhood's happy hour—that Ralph is really the Captain, and the Captain is Ralph?

BUT. That is the idea I intended to convey, officially!

SIR JOSEPH. And very well you have conveyed it.

BUT. Aye! aye! yer 'onour.

SIR JOSEPH. Dear me! Let them appear before me, at once!

RALPH *enters as* CAPTAIN; CAPTAIN *as a common sailor.* JOSEPHINE *rushes to his arms.*

JOS. My father—a common sailor!

CAPT. It is hard, is it not, my dear?

SIR JOSEPH. This is a very singular occurrence; I congratulate you both. (*To* RALPH.) Desire that remarkably fine seaman to step forward.

RALPH. Corcoran. Three paces to the front—march!

CAPT. If what?

RALPH. If what? I don't think I understand you.

CAPT. If you please.

SIR JOSEPH. The gentleman is quite right. If you *please.*

RALPH. Oh! If you *please.* (CAPTAIN *steps forward.*)

SIR JOSEPH (*to* CAPTAIN). You are an extremely fine fellow.

CAPT. Yes, your honour.

SIR JOSEPH. So it seems that you were Ralph, and Ralph was you.

CAPT. So it seems, your honour.

SIR JOSEPH. Well, I need not tell you that after this change in your condition, a marriage with your daughter will be out of the question.

CAPT. Don't say that, your honour—love levels all ranks.

SIR JOSEPH. It does to a considerable extent, but it does not level them as much as that. (*Handing* JOSEPHINE *to* RALPH.) Here—take her, sir, and mind you treat her kindly.

RALPH *and* JOS. Oh bliss, oh rapture!

CAPT. *and* BUT. Oh rapture, oh bliss!

SIR JOSEPH.   Sad my lot and sorry,
            What shall I do? I cannot live alone!

HEBE.   Fear nothing—while I live I'll not desert you.
            I'll soothe and comfort your declining days.

SIR JOSEPH.   No, don't do that.

HEBE.   Yes, but indeed I'd rather—

SIR JOSEPH (*resigned*). To-morrow morn our vows shall all be plighted,
            Three loving pairs on the same day united!

QUARTETTE

JOSEPHINE, HEBE, RALPH, *and* DEADEYE

Oh, joy, oh rapture unforeseen,
The clouded sky is now serene,
The god of day—the orb of love,
Has hung his ensign high above,
    The sky is all ablaze.
With wooing words and loving song,
We'll chase the lagging hours along,
And if $\left\{ \begin{array}{l} \text{he finds} \\ \text{I find} \end{array} \right\}$ the maiden coy,
We'll murmur forth decorous joy,
    In dreamy roundelay.

CAPT.   For he's the Captain of the *Pinafore*.

ALL.   And a right good captain too!

CAPT.   And though before my fall
            I was captain of you all,
I'm a member of the crew.

ALL.   Although before his fall, etc.

CAPT.   I shall marry with a wife,
            In my humble rank of life! (*turning to* BUT.)
            And you, my own, are she—
I must wander to and fro,
But wherever I may go,
            I shall never be untrue to thee!

ALL.   What, never?

CAPT.   No, never!

ALL.   What, *never*?

CAPT.   Hardly ever!

ALL.   Hardly ever be untrue to thee.
    Then give three cheers, and one cheer more
    For the former Captain of the *Pinafore*.

BUT.   For he loves Little Buttercup, dear Little Buttercup,
    Though I could never tell why;
    But still he loves Buttercup, poor Little Buttercup,
    Sweet Little Buttercup, aye!

ALL.   For he loves, etc.

SIR JOSEPH.   I'm the monarch of the sea,
    And when I've married thee (*to* HEBE)
    I'll be true to the devotion that my love implants,

HEBE.   Then good-bye to his sisters, and his cousins, and his aunts,
    Especially his cousins,
    Whom he reckons up by dozens,
    His sisters, and his cousins, and his aunts!

ALL.   For he is an Englishman,
    And he himself hath said it,
    And it's greatly to his credit
    That he is an Englishman!

CURTAIN

The Pirates of Penzance
OR
THE SLAVE OF DUTY

DRAMATIS PERSONÆ

MAJOR-GENERAL STANLEY.

THE PIRATE KING.

SAMUEL (*his Lieutenant*).

FREDERIC (*the Pirate Apprentice*).

SERGEANT OF POLICE.

MABEL
EDITH
KATE } (*General Stanley's Daughters*).
ISABEL

RUTH (*a Pirate Maid of all Work*).

Chorus of Pirates, Police, and General Stanley's Daughters

———

ACT I.—A Rocky Sea-shore on the Coast of Cornwall.

ACT II.—A Ruined Chapel by Moonlight.

First produced at the Opéra Comique on April 3, 1880.

The Pirates of Penzance

OR

THE SLAVE OF DUTY

ACT ONE

SCENE.—*A rocky sea-shore on the coast of Cornwall. In the distance is a calm sea, on which a schooner is lying at anchor. As the curtain rises groups of pirates are discovered—some drinking, some playing cards.* SAMUEL, *the Pirate Lieutenant, is going from one group to another, filling the cups from a flask.* FREDERIC *is seated in a despondent attitude at the back of the scene.*

OPENING CHORUS

Pour, oh, pour the pirate sherry;
Fill, oh, fill the pirate glass;
And, to make us more than merry,
Let the pirate bumper pass.

SAM. For to-day our pirate 'prentice
      Rises from indenture freed;
      Strong his arm and keen his scent is,
      He's a pirate now indeed!

ALL. Here's good luck to Frederic's ventures!
      Frederic's out of his indentures.

SAM. Two-and-twenty now he's rising,
      And alone he's fit to fly,
      Which we're bent on signalizing
      With unusual revelry.

ALL. Here's good luck to Frederic's ventures!
      Frederic's out of his indentures.
      Pour, oh, pour the pirate sherry, etc.

FREDERIC *rises and comes forward with* PIRATE KING, *who enters.*

KING. Yes, Frederic, from to-day you rank as a full-blown member of our band.

ALL. Hurrah!

FRED. My friends, I thank you all, from my heart, for your kindly wishes. Would that I could repay them as they deserve!

KING. What do you mean?

FRED. To-day I am out of my indentures, and to-day I leave you for ever.

KING. But this is quite unaccountable; a keener hand at scuttling a Cunarder or cutting out a P. & O. never shipped a handspike.

FRED. Yes, I have done my best for you. And why? It was my duty under my indentures, and I am the slave of duty. As a child I was regularly apprenticed to your band. It was through an error—no matter, the mistake was ours, not yours, and I was in honour bound by it.

SAM. An error? What error?

RUTH *enters*

FRED. I may not tell you; it would reflect upon my well-loved Ruth.

RUTH. Nay, dear master, my mind has long been gnawed by the cankering tooth of mystery. Better have it out at once.

SONG—RUTH

When Frederic was a little lad he proved so brave and daring,
His father thought he'd 'prentice him to some career seafaring.
I was, alas! his nurserymaid, and so it fell to *my* lot
To take and bind the promising boy apprentice to a *pilot*—
A life not bad for a hardy lad, though surely not a high lot,
Though I'm a nurse, you might do worse than make your boy a pilot.
I was a stupid nurserymaid, on breakers always steering,
And I did not catch the word aright, through being hard of hearing;
Mistaking my instructions, which within my brain did gyrate,
I took and bound this promising boy apprentice to a *pirate*.
A sad mistake it was to make and doom him to a vile lot.
I bound him to a pirate—you—instead of to a pilot.
I soon found out, beyond all doubt, the scope of this disaster,
But I hadn't the face to return to my place, and break it to my master.
A nurserymaid is not afraid of what you people *call* work,
So I made up my mind to go as a kind of piratical maid-of-all-work.
And that is how you find me now, a member of your shy lot,
Which you wouldn't have found, had he been bound apprentice to a
    pilot.

RUTH. Oh, pardon! Frederic, pardon! (*Kneels.*)
FRED. Rise, sweet one, I have long pardoned you.
RUTH (*rises*). The two words were so much alike!
FRED. They were. They still are, though years have rolled over their
heads. But this afternoon my obligation ceases. Individually, I love

you all with affection unspeakable, but, collectively, I look upon you with a disgust that amounts to absolute detestation. Oh! pity me, my beloved friends, for such is my sense of duty that, once out of my indentures, I shall feel myself bound to devote myself heart and soul to your extermination!

ALL. Poor lad—poor lad! (*All weep.*)

KING. Well, Frederic, if you conscientiously feel that it is your duty to destroy us, we cannot blame you for acting on that conviction. Always act in accordance with the dictates of your conscience, my boy, and chance the consequences.

SAM. Besides, we can offer you but little temptation to remain with us. We don't seem to make piracy pay. I'm sure I don't know why, but we don't.

FRED. *I* know why, but, alas! I mustn't tell you; it wouldn't be right.

KING. Why not, my boy? It's only half-past eleven, and you are one of us until the clock strikes twelve.

SAM. True, and until then you are bound to protect our interests.

ALL. Hear, hear!

FRED. Well, then, it is my duty, as a pirate, to tell you that you are too tender-hearted. For instance, you make a point of never attacking a weaker party than yourselves, and when you attack a stronger party you invariably get thrashed.

KING. There is some truth in that.

FRED. Then, again, you make a point of never molesting an orphan!

SAM. Of course: we are orphans ourselves, and know what it is.

FRED. Yes, but it has got about, and what is the consequence? Every one we capture says he's an orphan. The last three ships we took proved to be manned entirely by orphans, and so we had to let them go. One would think that Great Britain's mercantile navy was recruited solely from her orphan asylums—which we know is not the case.

SAM. But, hang it all! you wouldn't have us absolutely merciless?

FRED. There's my difficulty; until twelve o'clock I would, after twelve I wouldn't. Was ever a man placed in so delicate a situation?

RUTH. And Ruth, your own Ruth, whom you love so well, and who has won her middle-aged way into your boyish heart, what is to become of *her*?

KING. Oh, he will take you with him.

FRED. Well, Ruth, I feel some little difficulty about you. It is true that I admire you very much, but I have been constantly at sea since I was eight years old, and yours is the only woman's face I have seen during that time. I think it is a sweet face.

RUTH. It is—oh, it is!

FRED. I say I *think* it is; that is my impression. But as I have never had an opportunity of comparing you with other women, it is just possible I may be mistaken.

KING. True.

FRED. What a terrible thing it would be if I were to marry this innocent person, and then find out that she is, on the whole, plain!

KING. Oh, Ruth is very well, very well indeed.

SAM. Yes, there are the remains of a fine woman about Ruth.

FRED. Do you really think so?

SAM. I do.

FRED. Then I will not be so selfish as to take her from you. In justice to her, and in consideration for you, I will leave her behind. (*Hands* RUTH *to* KING.)

KING. No, Frederic, this must not be. We are rough men who lead a rough life, but we are not so utterly heartless as to deprive thee of thy love. I think I am right in saying that there is not one here who would rob thee of this inestimable treasure for all the world holds dear.

ALL (*loudly*). Not one!

KING. No, I thought there wasn't. Keep thy love, Frederic, keep thy love. (*Hands her back to* FREDERIC.)

FRED. You're very good, I'm sure. [*Exit* RUTH.

KING. Well, it's the top of the tide, and we must be off. Farewell, Frederic. When your process of extermination begins, let our deaths be as swift and painless as you can conveniently make them.

FRED. I will! By the love I have for you, I swear it! Would that you could render this extermination unnecessary by accompanying me back to civilization!

KING. No, Frederic, it cannot be. I don't think much of our profession, but, contrasted with respectability, it is comparatively honest. No, Frederic, I shall live and die a Pirate King.

SONG—PIRATE KING

Oh, better far to live and die
Under the brave black flag I fly,
Than play a sanctimonious part,
With a pirate head and a pirate heart.
Away to the cheating world go you,
Where pirates all are well-to-do;
But I'll be true to the song I sing,
And live and die a Pirate King.
    For I am a Pirate King.

ALL.   You are!
Hurrah for our Pirate King!

KING.   And it is, it is a glorious thing
To be a Pirate King.

ALL.   Hurrah!
Hurrah for our Pirate King!

KING.   When I sally forth to seek my prey
I help myself in a royal way:
I sink a few more ships, it's true,
Than a well-bred monarch ought to do;
But many a king on a first-class throne,
If he wants to call his crown his own,
Must manage somehow to get through
More dirty work than ever *I* do,
    Though I am a Pirate King.

ALL.   You are!
Hurrah for our Pirate King!

KING.   And it is, it is a glorious thing
To be a Pirate King!

ALL.   It is!
Hurrah for our Pirate King!

[Exeunt all except FREDERIC.

Enter RUTH.

RUTH. Oh, take me with you! I cannot live if I am left behind.

FRED. Ruth, I will be quite candid with you. You are very dear to me as you know, but I must be circumspect. You see, you are considerably older than I. A lad of twenty-one usually looks for a wife of seventeen.

64

RUTH. A wife of seventeen! You will find me a wife of a thousand!

FRED. No, but I shall find you a wife of forty-seven, and that is quite enough. Ruth, tell me candidly, and without reserve: compared with other women—how are *you?*

RUTH. I will answer you truthfully, master—I have a slight cold, but otherwise I am quite well.

FRED. I am sorry for your cold, but I was referring rather to your personal appearance. Compared with other women, are you beautiful?

RUTH (*bashfully*). I have been told so, dear master.

FRED. Ah, but lately?

RUTH. Oh, no, years and years ago.

FRED. What do you think of yourself?

RUTH. It is a delicate question to answer, but I think I am a fine woman.

FRED. That is your candid opinion?

RUTH. Yes, I should be deceiving you if I told you otherwise.

FRED. Thank you, Ruth, I believe you, for I am sure you would not practise on my inexperience; I wish to do the right thing, and if— I say *if*—you are really a fine woman, your age shall be no obstacle to our union! (*Chorus of Girls heard in the distance.*) Hark! Surely I hear voices! Who has ventured to approach our all but inaccessible lair? Can it be Custom House? No, it does not sound like Custom House.

RUTH (*aside*). Confusion! it is the voices of young girls! If he should see them I am lost.

FRED. (*looking off*). By all that's marvellous, a bevy of beautiful maidens!

RUTH (*aside*). Lost! lost! lost!

FRED. How lovely! how surpassingly lovely is the plainest of them! What grace—what delicacy—what refinement! And Ruth—Ruth told me she was beautiful!

RECIT.

FRED.   Oh, false one, you have deceived me!

RUTH.   I have deceived you?

FRED.   Yes, deceived me!

(*Denouncing her.*)

DUET—FRED. *and* RUTH

FRED. You told me you were fair as gold!

RUTH (*wildly*). And, master, am I not so?

FRED. And now I see you're plain and old.

RUTH. I am sure I am not a jot so.

FRED. Upon my innocence you play.

RUTH. I'm not the one to plot so.

FRED. Your face is lined, your hair is grey.

RUTH. It's gradually got so.

FRED. Faithless woman, to deceive me,
            I who trusted so!

RUTH. Master, master, do not leave me!
            Hear me, ere you go!
            My love without reflecting,
            Oh, do not be rejecting.
Take a maiden tender—her affection raw and green,
            At very highest rating,
            Has been accumulating
Summers seventeen—summers seventeen.
            Don't, beloved master,
            Crush me with disaster.
What is such a dower to the dower I have here?
            My love unabating
            Has been accumulating
Forty-seven year—forty-seven year!

ENSEMBLE

RUTH	FRED.
Don't, beloved master,	Yes, your former master
Crush me with disaster.	Saves you from disaster.
What is such a dower to the dower	Your love would be uncomfortably
I have here?	fervid, it is clear,
My love unabating	If, as you are stating,
Has been accumulating	It's been accumulating
Forty-seven year—forty-seven year!	Forty-seven year—forty-seven year!

[*At the end he renounces her, and she goes off in despair.*

RECIT.—FRED.

What shall I do? Before these gentle maidens
I dare not show in this alarming costume.
No, no, I must remain in close concealment
Until I can appear in decent clothing!

(Hides in cave as they enter climbing over the rocks.)

GIRLS.
Climbing over rocky mountain,
Skipping rivulet and fountain,
Passing where the willows quiver
By the ever-rolling river,
    Swollen with the summer rain;
Threading long and leafy mazes
Dotted with unnumbered daisies;
Scaling rough and rugged passes,
Climb the hardy little lasses,
    Till the bright sea-shore they gain!

EDITH.
Let us gaily tread the measure,
Make the most of fleeting leisure;
Hail it as a true ally,
Though it perish by and by.

ALL.
    Hail it as a true ally,
    Though it perish by and by.

EDITH.
Every moment brings a treasure
Of its own especial pleasure,
Though the moments quickly die,
Greet them gaily as they fly.

KATE.
Far away from toil and care,
Revelling in fresh sea air,
Here we live and reign alone
In a world that's all our own.
Here in this our rocky den,
Far away from mortal men,
We'll be queens, and make decrees—
They may honour them who please.

ALL.
Let us gaily tread the measure, etc.

KATE. What a picturesque spot! I wonder where we are!

EDITH. And I wonder where papa is. We have left him ever so far
behind.

ISABEL. Oh, he will be here presently! Remember poor papa is not as young as we are, and we have come over a rather difficult country.

KATE. But how thoroughly delightful it is to be so entirely alone! Why, in all probability we are the first human beings who ever set foot on this enchanting spot.

ISABEL. Except the mermaids—it's the very place for mermaids.

KATE. Who are only human beings down to the waist!

EDITH. And who can't be said strictly to set *foot* anywhere. Tails they may, but feet they *cannot*.

KATE. But what shall we do until papa and the servants arrive with the luncheon?

EDITH. We are quite alone, and the sea is as smooth as glass. Suppose we take off our shoes and stockings and paddle?

ALL. Yes, yes! The very thing! (*They prepare to carry out the suggestion. They have all taken off one shoe, when* FREDERIC *comes forward from cave.*)

FRED. (*recitative*).   Stop, ladies, pray!
ALL (*hopping on one foot*).   A man!
FRED.   I had intended
  Not to intrude myself upon your notice
  In this effective but alarming costume,
  But under these peculiar circumstances
  It is my bounden duty to inform you
  That your proceedings will not be unwitnessed!
EDITH.   But who are you, sir? Speak!   (*All hopping.*)
FRED.   I am a pirate!
ALL (*recoiling, hopping*).   A pirate! Horror!
FRED.   Ladies, do not shun me!
  This evening I renounce my wild profession;
  And to that end, oh, pure and peerless maidens!
  Oh, blushing buds of ever-blooming beauty!
  I, sore at heart, implore your kind assistance.
EDITH.   How pitiful his tale!
KATE.   How rare his beauty
ALL.   How pitiful his tale! How rare his beauty!

SONG—FRED.

Oh, is there not one maiden breast
   Which does not feel the moral beauty
Of making worldly interest
   Subordinate to sense of duty?
Who would not give up willingly
   All matrimonial ambition,
To rescue such a one as I
   From his unfortunate position?

ALL.

Alas! there's not one maiden breast
   Which seems to feel the moral beauty
Of making worldly interest
   Subordinate to sense of duty!

FRED.

Oh, is there not one maiden here
   Whose homely face and bad complexion
Have caused all hopes to disappear
   Of ever winning man's affection?
To such a one, if such there be,
   I swear by Heaven's arch above you,
If you will cast your eyes on me—
   However plain you be—I'll love you!

ALL.

Alas! there's not one maiden here
   Whose homely face and bad complexion
Have caused all hope to disappear
   Of ever winning man's affection!

FRED. (*in despair*). Not one?

ALL.   No, no—not one!

FRED. Not one?

ALL.   No, no!

MABEL *enters.*

MABEL.   Yes, one!

ALL. 'Tis Mabel!

MABEL. Yes, 'tis Mabel!

RECIT.—MABEL

Oh, sisters, deaf to pity's name,
         For shame!

It's true that he has gone astray,
But pray
Is that a reason good and true
Why you
Should all be deaf to pity's name?

ALL (*aside*).   The question is, had he not been
A thing of beauty?
Would she be swayed by quite as keen
A sense of duty?

MABEL.   For shame, for shame, for shame!

SONG—MABEL

Poor wandering one!
Though thou hast surely strayed,
Take heart of grace,
Thy steps retrace,
Poor wandering one!
Poor wandering one!
If such poor love as mine
Can help thee find
True peace of mind—

70

Why, take it, it is thine!
Take heart, fair days will shine;
Take any heart—take mine!

ALL.
Take heart; no danger lowers;
Take any heart—but ours!

[*Exeunt* MABEL *and* FREDERIC.

(EDITH *beckons her sisters, who form in a semicircle around her.*)

EDITH

What ought we to do,
Gentle sisters, say?
Propriety, we know,
Says we ought to stay;
While sympathy exclaims,
"Free them from your tether—
Play at other games—
Leave them here together."

KATE

Her case may, any day,
Be yours, my dear, or mine.
Let her make her hay
While the sun doth shine.
Let us compromise,
(Our hearts are not of leather.)
Let us shut our eyes,
And talk about the weather.

GIRLS.
Yes, yes, let's talk about the weather.

CHATTERING CHORUS

How beautifully blue the sky,
The glass is rising very high,
Continue fine I hope it may,
And yet it rained but yesterday.
To-morrow it may pour again
(I hear the country wants some rain),
Yet people say, I know not why,
That we shall have a warm July.

W. S. GILBERT

Enter MABEL *and* FREDERIC.

(During MABEL's *solo the Girls continue chatter pianissimo, but listening eagerly all the time.)*

SOLO—MABEL

Did ever maiden wake
From dream of homely duty,
To find her daylight break
With such exceeding beauty?
Did ever maiden close
Her eyes on waking sadness,
To dream of such exceeding gladness?

FRED. Oh, yes! ah, yes! this is exceeding gladness.

GIRLS. How beautifully blue the sky, etc.

SOLO—FRED.

(During this, Girls continue their chatter pianissimo as before, but listening intently all the time.)

Did ever pirate roll
His soul in guilty dreaming,
And wake to find that soul
With peace and virtue beaming?

ENSEMBLE

MABEL.	FRED.	GIRLS
Did ever maiden wake, etc.	Did ever pirate roll, etc.	How beautifully blue the sky, etc.

RECIT.—FRED.

Stay, we must not lose our senses;
Men who stick at no offences
Will anon be here.
Piracy their dreadful trade is;
Pray you, get you hence, young ladies,
While the coast is clear.

[FREDERIC *and* MABEL *retire.*

GIRLS.	No, we must not lose our senses,
If they stick at no offences
We should not be here.
Piracy their dreadful trade is—
Nice companions for young ladies!
Let us disappear.

During this chorus the Pirates have entered stealthily, and formed in a semicircle behind the Girls. As the Girls move to go off each Pirate seizes a girl. KING *seizes* EDITH *and* ISABEL, SAMUEL *seizes* KATE.

ALL.	Too late!
PIRATES.	Ha! Ha!
ALL.	Too late!
PIRATES.	Ha! Ha!
Ha! ha! ha! ha! Ha! ha! ha! ha!

ENSEMBLE

(*Pirates pass in front of Girls.*)	(*Girls pass in front of Pirates.*)

PIRATES	GIRLS
Here's a first-rate opportunity	We have missed our opportunity
To get married with impunity,	Of escaping with impunity;
And indulge in the felicity	So farewell to the felicity
Of unbounded domesticity.	Of our maiden domesticity!
You shall quickly be parsonified,	We shall quicky be parsonified,
Conjugally matrimonified,	Conjugally matrimonified,
By a doctor of divinity,	By a doctor of divinity,
Who resides in this vicinity.	Who resides in this vicinity.

MABEL (*coming forward*).

RECIT.

Hold, monsters! Ere your pirate caravanserai
Proceed, against our will, to wed us all,
Just bear in mind that we are Wards in Chancery,
And father is a Major-General!
SAM. (*cowed*). We'd better pause, or danger may befall,
Their father is a Major-General.

73

GIRLS.   Yes, yes; he is a Major-General!

The MAJOR-GENERAL *has entered unnoticed, on rock.*

GEN.   Yes, I am a Major-General!
SAM.   For he is a Major-General!
ALL.   He is!   Hurrah for the Major-General!
GEN.   And it is—it is a glorious thing
    To be a Major-General!
ALL.   It is!   Hurrah for the Major-General!

SONG—MAJOR-GENERAL

I am the very model of a modern Major-Gineral,
I've information vegetable, animal, and mineral,
I know the kings of England, and I quote the fights historical,
From Marathon to Waterloo, in order categorical;
I'm very well acquainted too with matters mathematical,
I understand equations, both the simple and quadratical,
About binomial theorem I'm teeming with a lot o' news—
With many cheerful facts about the square of the hypotenuse.
ALL. With many cheerful facts, etc.
GEN. I'm very good at integral and differential calculus,
I know the scientific names of beings animalculous;
In short, in matters vegetable, animal, and mineral,
I am the very model of a modern Major-Gineral.

ALL. In short, in matters vegetable, animal, and mineral,
He is the very model of a modern Major-Gineral.

GEN. I know our mythic history, King Arthur's and Sir Caradoc's,
I answer hard acrostics, I've a pretty taste for paradox,
I quote in elegiacs all the crimes of Heliogabalus,
In conics I can floor peculiarities parabolous.
I can tell undoubted Raphaels from Gerard Dows and Zoffanies,
I know the croaking chorus from the *Frogs* of Aristophanes,
Then I can hum a fugue of which I've heard the music's din afore,
And whistle all the airs from that infernal nonsense *Pinafore*.

ALL. And whistle all the airs, etc.

GEN. Then I can write a washing bill in Babylonic cuneiform,
And tell you every detail of Caractacus's uniform;
In short, in matters vegetable, animal, and mineral,
I am the very model of a modern Major-Gineral.

ALL. In short, in matters vegetable, animal, and mineral,
He is the very model of a modern Major-Gineral.

GEN. In fact, when I know what is meant by "mamelon" and "ravelin,"
When I can tell at sight a chassepôt rifle from a javelin,
When such affairs as sorties and surprises I'm more wary at,
And when I know precisely what is meant by "commissariat",
When I have learnt what progress has been made in modern
gunnery,
When I know more of tactics than a novice in a nunnery;
In short, when I've a smattering of elemental strategy,
You'll say a better Major-Gener*al* has never *sat* a gee—

ALL. You'll say a better, etc.

GEN. For my military knowledge, though I'm plucky and adventury,
Has only been brought down to the beginning of the century;
But still in matters vegetable, animal, and mineral,
I am the very model of a modern Major-Gineral.

ALL. But still in matters vegetable, animal, and mineral.
He is the very model of a modern Major-Gineral.

GEN. And now that I've introduced myself I should like to have some idea of what's going on.

KATE. Oh, papa—we——

SAM. Permit me, I'll explain in two words: we propose to marry your daughters.

GEN. Dear me!

GIRLS. Against our wills, papa—against our wills!

GEN. Oh, but you mustn't do that! May I ask—this is a picturesque uniform, but I'm not familiar with it. What are you?

KING. We are all single gentlemen.

GEN. Yes, I gathered that—anything else?

KING. No, nothing else.

EDITH. Papa, don't believe them; they are pirates—the famous Pirates of Penzance!

GEN. The Pirates of Penzance! I have often heard of them.

MABEL. All except this gentleman—(*indicating* FREDERIC)—who was a pirate once, but who is out of his indentures to-day, and who means to lead a blameless life evermore.

GEN. But wait a bit. I object to pirates as sons-in-law.

KING. We object to Major-Generals as fathers-in-law. But we waive that point. We do not press it. We look over it.

GEN. (*aside*). Hah! an idea! (*Aloud*.) And do you mean to say that you would deliberately rob me of these, the sole remaining props of my old age, and leave me to go through the remainder of my life unfriended, unprotected, and alone?

KING. Well, yes, that's the idea.

GEN. Tell me, have you ever known what it is to be an orphan?

PIRATES (*disgusted*). Oh, dash it all!

KING. Here we are again!

GEN. I ask you, have you ever known what it is to be an orphan?

KING. Often!

GEN. Yes, orphan. Have you ever known what it is to be one?

KING. I say, often.

ALL (*disgusted*). Often, often, often. (*Turning away*.)

GEN. I don't think we quite understand one another. I ask you, have you ever known what it is to be an orphan, and you say "orphan". As I understand you, you are merely repeating the word "orphan" to show that you understand me.

KING. I didn't repeat the word often.

GEN. Pardon me, you did indeed.

KING. I only repeated it once.

GEN. True, but you repeated it.

KING. But not often.

GEN. Stop: I think I see where we are getting confused. When you said "orphan", did you mean "orphan"—a person who has lost his parents, or "often"—frequently?

KING. Ah! I beg pardon—I see what you mean—frequently.

GEN. Ah! you said often—frequently.

KING. No, only once.

GEN. (*irritated*). Exactly—you said often, frequently, only once.

RECIT.—GENERAL

Oh, men of dark and dismal fate,
Forgo your cruel employ,
Have pity on my lonely state,
I am an orphan boy!

KING *and* SAM. An orphan boy?
GEN. An orphan boy!
PIRATES. How sad—an orphan boy.

SOLO—GENERAL

These children whom you see
Are all that I can call my own!
PIRATES. Poor fellow!
GEN. Take them away from me
And I shall be indeed alone.
PIRATES. Poor fellow!
GEN. If pity you can feel,
Leave me my sole remaining joy—
See, at your feet they kneel;
Your hearts you cannot steel
Against the sad, sad tale of the lonely orphan boy!
PIRATES (*sobbing*). Poor fellow!
See at our feet they kneel;
Our hearts we cannot steel
Against the sad, sad tale of the lonely orphan boy!
KING. The orphan boy!
SAM. The orphan boy!
ALL. The lonely orphan boy! Poor fellow!

ENSEMBLE

GENERAL (*aside*)

I'm telling a terrible story,

But it doesn't diminish my glory;
For they would have taken my daughters
Over the billowy waters,

GIRLS (*aside*)

He's telling a terrible story,

Which will tend to diminish his glory;
Though they would have taken his daughters
Over the billowy waters.

PIRATES (*aside*)

If he's telling a terrible story,

He shall die by a death that is gory,
One of the cruellest slaughters
That ever were known in these waters;

GENERAL (*aside*)

If I hadn't, in elegant diction,
Indulged in an innocent fiction;
Which is not in the same category
As a regular terrible story.

GIRLS (*aside*)

It's easy, in elegant diction,
To call it an innocent fiction,
But it comes in the same category
As a regular terrible story.

PIRATES (*aside*)

And we'll finish his moral affliction
By a very complete malediction,
As a compliment valedictory,
If he's telling a terrible story.

KING

Although our dark career
   Sometimes involves the crime of stealing,
We rather think that we're
   Not altogether void of feeling.
Although we live by strife,
   We're always sorry to begin it,
For what, we ask, is life
   Without a touch of Poetry in it?

ALL (*kneeling*)

Hail, Poetry, thou heaven-born maid!
Thou gildest e'en the pirate's trade:
Hail, flowing fount of sentiment!
All hail, Divine Emollient! (*All rise.*)

KING

You may go, for you're at liberty, our pirate rules protect you,
And honorary members of our band we do elect you.

SAM.   For he is an orphan boy.

CHORUS.   He is! Hurrah for the orphan boy.

GEN.   And it sometimes is a useful thing
            To be an orphan boy.

78

CHORUS.   It is! Hurrah for the orphan boy!
            Oh, happy day, with joyous glee
            They will away and married be;
            Should it befall auspiciously,
            Our sisters all will bridesmaids be!

RUTH *enters and comes down to* FREDERIC.

RUTH.   Oh, master, hear one word, I do implore you!
            Remember Ruth, your Ruth, who kneels before you!
CHORUS.   Yes, yes, remember Ruth, who kneels before you!
FRED.   (*Pirates threaten* RUTH.) Away, you did deceive me!
CHORUS.   Away, you did deceive him!
RUTH.   Oh, do not leave me!
CHORUS.   Oh, do not leave her!
FRED.   Away, you grieve me!
CHORUS.   Away, you grieve him!
FRED.   I wish you'd leave me!

            (FREDERIC *casts* RUTH *from him.*)

CHORUS.   We wish you'd leave him!

ENSEMBLE

Pray observe the magnanimity
We ⎱
They ⎰ display to lace and dimity!
Never was such opportunity
To get married with impunity,
But ⎰ we ⎱ give up the felicity
    ⎱ they ⎰
Of unbounded domesticity,
Though a doctor of divinity
Resides in this vicinity.

[*Girls and* GENERAL *go up rocks, while Pirates indulge
in a wild dance of delight on stage. The* GENERAL
produces a British flag, and the PIRATE KING *produces a black flag with skull and cross-bones.
Enter* RUTH, *who makes a final appeal to* FREDERIC,
who casts her from him.

END OF ACT I

79

ACT TWO

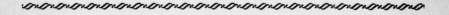

SCENE.—*A Ruined Chapel by Moonlight. Ruined Gothic windows at back.* GENERAL STANLEY *discovered seated pensively, surrounded by his daughters.*

CHORUS

Oh, dry the glistening tear
  That dews that martial cheek;
Thy loving children hear,
  In them thy comfort seek.
With sympathetic care
  Their arms around thee creep,
For oh, they cannot bear
  To see their father weep!

Enter MABEL.

SOLO—MABEL

Dear father, why leave your bed
  At this untimely hour,
When happy daylight is dead,
  And darksome dangers lower?
See, heaven has lit her lamp,
  The midnight hour is past,
The chilly night air is damp,
  And the dews are falling fast!
Dear father, why leave your bed
When happy daylight is dead?

FREDERIC *enters.*

MABEL. Oh, Frederic, cannot you, in the calm excellence of your wisdom, reconcile it with your conscience to say something that will relieve my father's sorrow?

FRED. I will try, dear Mabel. But why does he sit, night after night, in this draughty old ruin?

GEN. Why do I sit here? To escape from the pirates' clutches, I described myself as an orphan, and, heaven help me, I am no orphan! I come here to humble myself before the tombs of my ancestors, and to implore their pardon for having brought dishonour on the family escutcheon.

FRED. But you forget, sir, you only bought the property a year ago, and the stucco in your baronial hall is scarcely dry.

GEN. Frederic, in this chapel are ancestors: you cannot deny that. With the estate, I bought the chapel and its contents. I don't know whose ancestors they *were,* but I know whose ancestors they *are,* and I shudder to think that their descendant by purchase (if I may so describe myself) should have brought disgrace upon what, I have no doubt, was an unstained escutcheon.

FRED. Be comforted. Had you not acted as you did, these reckless men would assuredly have called in the nearest clergyman, and have married your large family on the spot.

GEN. I thank you for your proffered solace, but it is unavailing. I assure you, Frederic, that such is the anguish and remorse I feel at the abominable falsehood by which I escaped these easily deluded pirates, that I would go to their simple-minded chief this very night and confess all, did I not fear that the consequences would be most disastrous to myself. At what time does your expedition march against these scoundrels?

FRED. At eleven, and before midnight I hope to have atoned for my involuntary association with the pestilent scourges by sweeping them from the face of the earth—and then, dear Mabel, you will be mine!

GEN. Are your devoted followers at hand?

FRED. They are, they only wait my orders.

W. S. GILBERT

RECITATIVE—GENERAL

Then, Frederic, let your escort lion-hearted
Be summoned to receive a General's blessing,
Ere they depart upon their dread adventure.
Dear sir, they come.

Enter Police, marching in single file. They form in line, facing audience.

SONG—SERGEANT

When the foeman bares his steel,
Tarantara! tarantara!
We uncomfortable feel,
Tarantara!
And we find the wisest thing,
Tarantara! tarantara!
Is to slap our chests and sing
Tarantara!
For when threatened with emeutes,
Tarantara! tarantara!
And your heart is in your boots,
Tarantara!
There is nothing brings it round,
Tarantara! tarantara!
Like the trumpet's martial sound,
Tarantara! tarantara!
Tarantara-ra-ra-ra-ra!

ALL. Tarantara-ra-ra-ra-ra!
MABEL. Go, ye heroes, go to glory,
Though you die in combat gory,
Ye shall live in song and story.
Go to immortality!
Go to death, and go to slaughter;
Die, and every Cornish daughter
With her tears your grave shall water.
Go, ye heroes, go and die!
ALL. Go, ye heroes, go and die!

POLICE

Though to us it's evident,
    Tarantara! tarantara!
These intentions are well meant,
    Tarantara!
Such expressions don't appear,
    Tarantara! tarantara!
Calculated men to cheer,
    Tarantara!
Who are going to meet their fate
In a highly nervous state,
    Tarantara!
Still to us it's evident
These intentions are well meant.
    Tarantara!

EDITH.

Go and do your best endeavour,
And before all links we sever,
We will say farewell for ever.
   Go to glory and the grave!

GIRLS.

For your foes are fierce and ruthless,
False, unmerciful, and truthless.
Young and tender, old and toothless,
   All in vain their mercy crave.

SERG.

We observe too great a stress,
On the risks that on us press,
And of reference a lack
To our chance of coming back.
Still, perhaps it would be wise
Not to carp or criticise,
For it's very evident
These attentions are well meant.

ALL.

Yes, to them it's evident
Our attentions are well meant.
    Tarantara-ra-ra-ra-ra!
Go, ye heroes, go to glory, etc.

83

ENSEMBLE

Chorus of all but Police	*Chorus of Police*
Go and do your best endeavour,	Such expressions don't appear,
And before all links we sever	Tarantara, tarantara!
We will say farewell for ever.	Calculated men to cheer,
Go to glory and the grave!	Tarantara!
For your foes are fierce and ruthless,	Who are going to their fate,
False, unmerciful, and truthless.	Tarantara, tarantara!
Young and tender, old and toothless,	In a highly nervous state—
All in vain their mercy crave.	Tarantara!
	We observe too great a stress,
	Tarantara, tarantara!
	On the risks that on us press,
	Tarantara!
	And of reference a lack,
	Tarantara, tarantara!
	To our chance of coming back.
	Tarantara!

GEN.   Away, away!

POLICE (*without moving*).   Yes, yes, we go.

GEN.   These pirates slay.

POLICE.   Tarantara!

GEN.   Then do not stay.

POLICE.   Tarantara!

GEN.   Then why this delay?

POLICE.   All right—we go.

           Yes, forward on the foe!

GEN.   Yes, but you *don't* go!

POLICE.   We go, we go!

           Yes, forward on the foe!

GEN.   Yes, but you *don't* go!

ALL.   At last they really go.

[MABEL *tears herself from* FREDERIC *and exit, followed
    by her sisters, consoling her. The* GENERAL *and
    others follow.* FREDERIC *remains.*

RECITATIVE—FREDERIC

Now for the pirates' lair! Oh, joy unbounded!
Oh, sweet relief! Oh, rapture unexampled!

At last I may atone, in some slight measure,
For the repeated acts of theft and pillage
Which, at a sense of duty's stern dictation,
I, circumstance's victim, have been guilty.

(KING *and* RUTH *appear at the window, armed.*)

KING. Young Frederic! (*Covering him with pistol.*)
FRED. Who calls?
KING. Your late commander!
RUTH. And I, your little Ruth! (*Covering him with pistol.*)
FRED. Oh, mad intruders,
How dare ye face me? Know ye not, oh rash ones,
That I have doomed you to extermination?

(KING *and* RUTH *hold a pistol to each ear.*)

KING. Have mercy on us, hear us, ere you slaughter.
FRED. I do not think I ought to listen to you.
Yet, mercy should alloy our stern resentment,
And so I will be merciful—say on!

TRIO—RUTH, KING, *and* FRED.

RUTH. When you had left our pirate fold
We tried to raise our spirits faint,
According to our customs old,
With quips and quibbles quaint.
But all in vain the quips we heard,
We lay and sobbed upon the rocks,
Until to somebody occurred
A startling paradox.
FRED. A paradox?
KING (*laughing*). A paradox!
RUTH. A most ingenious paradox!
We've quips and quibbles heard in flocks,
But none to beat this paradox!
Ha! ha! ha! ha! Ho! ho! ho! ho!
KING. We knew your taste for curious quips,
For cranks and contradictions queer,
And with the laughter on our lips,
We wished you there to hear.

We said, "If we could tell it him,
  How Frederic would the joke enjoy!"
And so we've risked both life and limb
  To tell it to our boy.

FRED. (*interested*). That paradox? That paradox?

KING
and } (*laughing*). That most ingenious paradox!
RUTH

We've quips and quibbles heard in flocks,
  But none to beat that paradox!
  Ha! ha! ha! ha! Ho! ho! ho! ho!

CHANT—KING

For some ridiculous reason, to which, however, I've no desire to be disloyal,

Some person in authority, I don't know who, very likely the Astronomer Royal,

Has decided that, although for such a beastly month as February, twenty-eight days as a rule are plenty,

One year in every four his days shall be reckoned as nine-and-twenty.

Through some singular coincidence—I shouldn't be surprised if it were owing to the agency of an ill-natured fairy—

You are the victim of this clumsy arrangement, having been born in leap-year, on the twenty-ninth of February,

And so, by a simple arithmetical process, you'll easily discover,

That though you've lived twenty-one years, yet, if we go by birthdays, you're only five and a little bit over!

RUTH.	Ha! ha! ha! ha!
KING.	Ho! ho! ho! ho!
FRED.	Dear me!
	Let's see! (*counting on fingers*).
	Yes, yes; with yours my figures do agree!
ALL.	Ha! ha! ha! ha! Ho! ho! ho! ho! (FREDERIC *more amused than any.*)
FRED.	How quaint the ways of Paradox!
	At common sense she gaily mocks!
	Though counting in the usual way,
	Years twenty-one I've been alive,

86

Yet, reckoning by my natal day,
   I am a little boy of five!

ALL.   He is a little boy of five! Ha! ha!
A paradox, a paradox,
A most ingenious paradox!
Ha! ha! ha! ha! Ho! ho! ho! ho! (RUTH *and* KING
   throw themselves back on seats, exhausted with
   laughter.)

FRED. Upon my word, this is most curious—most absurdly whimsical. Five-and-a-quarter! No one would think it to look at me!

RUTH. You are glad now, I'll be bound, that you spared us. You would never have forgiven yourself when you discovered that you had killed *two of your comrades.*

FRED. My comrades?

KING (*rises*). I'm afraid you don't appreciate the delicacy of your position. You were apprenticed to us——

FRED. Until I reached my twenty-first year.

KING. No, until you reached your twenty-first *birthday* (*producing document*), and, going by birthdays, you are as yet only five-and-a-quarter.

FRED. You don't mean to say you are going to hold me to that?

KING. No, we merely remind you of the fact, and leave the rest to your sense of duty.

RUTH. Your sense of duty!

FRED. (*wildly*). Don't put it on that footing! As I was merciful to you just now, be merciful to me! I implore you not to insist on the letter of your bond just as the cup of happiness is at my lips!

RUTH. We insist on nothing; we content ourselves with pointing out to you *your duty.*

KING. Your duty!

FRED. (*after a pause*). Well, you have appealed to my sense of duty, and my duty is only too clear. I abhor your infamous calling; I shudder at the thought that I have ever been mixed up with it; but duty is before all—at any price I will do my duty.

KING. Bravely spoken! Come, you are one of us once more.

FRED. Lead on, I follow. (*Suddenly.*) Oh, horror!

87

KING.
RUTH. } What is the matter?

FRED. Ought I to tell you? No, no, I cannot do it; and yet, as one of your band——

KING. Speak out, I charge you by that sense of conscientiousness to which we have never yet appealed in vain.

FRED. General Stanley, the father of my Mabel——

KING.
RUTH. } Yes, yes!

FRED. He escaped from you on the plea that he was an orphan!

KING. He did!

FRED. It breaks my heart to betray the honoured father of the girl I adore, but as your apprentice I have no alternative. It is my duty to tell you that General Stanley is no orphan!

KING.
RUTH. } What!

FRED. More than that, he never was one!

KING. Am I to understand that, to save his contemptible life, he dared to practise on our credulous simplicity? (FREDERIC *nods as he weeps.*) Our revenge shall be swift and terrible. We will go and collect our band and attack Tremorden Castle this very night.

FRED. But—stay——

KING. Not a word! He is doomed!

TRIO

KING *and* RUTH   FREDERIC

Away, away! my heart's on fire,   Away, away! ere I expire—
  I burn this base deception to re-   I find my duty hard to do to-day!
    pay,   My heart is filled with anguish dire,
This very night my vengeance dire   It strikes me to the core. Away,
  Shall glut itself in gore. Away,   away!
    away!

KING

With falsehood foul
He tricked us of our brides.
Let vengeance howl;
The Pirate so decides.

88

                    Our nature stern
                    He softened with his lies,
                        And, in return,
                    To-night the traitor dies.
ALL.   Yes, yes! to-night the traitor dies.
RUTH.   To-night he dies!
KING.   Yes, or early to-morrow.
FRED.   His girls likewise?
RUTH.   They will welter in sorrow.
KING.   The one soft spot
FRED.   In their natures they cherish—
RUTH.   And all who plot
KING.   To abuse it shall perish!
ALL.   Yes, all who plot
                    To abuse it shall perish!
                    Away, away! etc.

                                        [*Exeunt* KING *and* RUTH.

          Enter MABEL.

                    RECIT.—MABEL

All is prepared, your gallant crew await you.
My Frederic in tears? It cannot be
That lion-heart quails at the coming conflict?
FRED.   No, Mabel, no. A terrible disclosure
Has just been made! Mabel, my dearly-loved one,
I bound myself to serve the pirate captain
Until I reached my one-and-twentieth birthday—
MABEL.   But you *are* twenty-one?
FRED.   I've just discovered
That I was born in leap-year, and that birthday
Will not be reached by me till 1940.
MABEL.   Oh, horrible! catastrophe appalling!
FRED.   And so, farewell!!
MABEL.   No, no! Ah, Frederic, hear me.

                    DUET—MABEL *and* FRED.

MABEL.   Stay, Frederic, stay!
                        They have no legal claim,

No shadow of a shame
    Will fall upon thy name.
Stay, Frederic, stay!

FRED.　　Nay, Mabel, nay!
    To-night I quit these walls,
    The thought my soul appals,
    But when stern Duty calls,
I must obey.

MABEL.　　Stay, Frederic, stay!

FRED.　　Nay, Mabel, nay!

MABEL.　　They have no claim—

FRED.　　But Duty's name!
    The thought my soul appals,
    But when stern Duty calls,
I must obey.

BALLAD—MABEL

Ah, leave me not to pine
    Alone and desolate;
No fate seemed fair as mine,
    No happiness so great!
And nature, day by day,
    Has sung, in accents clear,
This joyous roundelay,
    "He loves thee—he is here.
        Fa-la, fa-la, fa-la."

FRED.　　Ah, must I leave thee here
    In endless night to dream,
Where joy is dark and drear,
    And sorrow all supreme!
Where nature, day by day,
    Will sing, in altered tone.
This weary roundelay,
    "He loves thee—he is gone.
        Fa-la, fa-la, fa-la."

FRED.　　In 1940 I of age shall be,
I'll then return, and claim you—I declare it!

MABEL.   It seems so long!

FRED.   Swear that, till then, you will be true to me.

MABEL.   Yes, I'll be strong!
By all the Stanleys dead and gone, I swear it!

ENSEMBLE

Oh, here is love, and here is truth,
And here is food for joyous laughter.

He / She } will be faithful to { his / her } sooth

Till we are wed, and even after.

[FREDERIC *rushes to window and leaps out.*

MABEL (*almost fainting*). No, I am brave! Oh, family descent,
How great thy charm, thy sway how excellent!
Come, one and all, undaunted men in blue,
A crisis, now, affairs are coming to!

Enter Police, marching in single file.

SERG.   Though in body and in mind,
Tarantara, tarantara!
We are timidly inclined,
Tarantara!
And anything but blind,
Tarantara, tarantara!
To the danger that's behind,
Tarantara!
Yet, when the danger's near,
Tarantara, tarantara!
We manage to appear,
Tarantara!
As insensible to fear
As anybody here.
Tarantara, tarantara-ra-ra-ra-ra!

MABEL. Sergeant, approach! Young Frederic was to have led you to death and glory.

ALL. That is not a pleasant way of putting it.

MABEL. No matter; he will not so lead you, for he has allied himself once more with his old associates.

ALL. He has acted shamefully!

MABEL. You speak falsely. You know nothing about it. He has acted nobly.

ALL. He has acted nobly!

MABEL. Dearly as I loved him before, his heroic sacrifice to his sense of duty has endeared him to me tenfold. He has done his duty. I will do mine. Go ye and do yours.   [*Exit* MABEL.

ALL. Right oh!

SERG. This is perplexing.

ALL. We cannot understand it at all.

SERG. Still, as he is actuated by a sense of duty——

ALL. That makes a difference, of course. At the same time we repeat, we cannot understand it at all.

SERG. No matter; our course is clear. We must do our best to capture these pirates alone. It is most distressing to us to be the agents whereby our erring fellow-creatures are deprived of that liberty which is so dear to all—but we should have thought of that before we joined the Force.

ALL. We should!

SERG. It is too late now!

ALL. It is!

SONG—SERGEANT

SERG.   When a felon's not engaged in his employment—

ALL.   His employment,

SERG.   Or maturing his felonious little plans—

ALL.   Little plans,

SERG.   His capacity for innocent enjoyment—

ALL.   'Cent enjoyment

SERG.   Is just as great as any honest man's—

ALL.   Honest man's.

SERG.   Our feelings we with difficulty smother—

ALL.   'Culty smother

SERG.   When constabulary duty's to be done—

ALL.   To be done.

SERG.   Ah, take one consideration with another—

ALL.   With another,

SERG.   A policeman's lot is not a happy one

92

ALL.
When constabulary duty's to be done—
To be done,
The policeman's lot is not a happy one.

SERG. When the enterprising burglar's not a-burgling—
ALL. Not a-burgling,
SERG. When the cut-throat isn't occupied in crime—
ALL. 'Pied in crime,
SERG. He loves to hear the little brook a-gurgling—
ALL. Brook a-gurgling,
SERG. And listen to the merry village chime—
ALL. Village chime.
SERG. When the coster's finished jumping on his mother—
ALL. On his mother,
SERG. He loves to lie a-basking in the sun—
ALL. In the sun.
SERG. Ah, take one consideration with another—
ALL. With another,
SERG. The policeman's lot is not a happy one.
ALL. When constabulary duty's to be done—
To be done,
The policeman's lot is not a happy one—
Happy one.

(*Chorus of Pirates without, in the distance.*)

A rollicking band of pirates we,
Who, tired of tossing on the sea,
Are trying their hand at a burglaree,
With weapons grim and gory.

SERG. Hush, hush! I hear them on the manor poaching,
   With stealthy step the pirates are approaching.

(Chorus of Pirates, resumed nearer.)

   We are not coming for plate or gold—
   A story General Stanley's told—
   We seek a penalty fifty-fold,
    For General Stanley's story.

POLICE. They seek a penalty—
PIRATES (*without*).   Fifty-fold,
   We seek a penalty—
POLICE.   Fifty-fold,

ALL. We }
  They } seek a penalty fifty-fold,
   For General Stanley's story.

SERG. They come in force, with stealthy stride,
   Our obvious course is now—to hide.

Police conceal themselves. As they do so, the Pirates are seen appearing at ruined window. They enter cautiously, and come down stage. SAMUEL is laden with burglarious tools and pistols, etc.

CHORUS—PIRATES (*very loud*)

   With cat-like tread,
    Upon our prey we steal,
   In silence dread
    Our cautious way we feel.
   No sound at all,
    We never speak a word,
   A fly's foot-fall
    Would be distinctly heard—

POLICE (*pianissimo*).   Tarantara, tarantara!
PIRATES. So stealthily the pirate creeps,
   While all the household soundly sleeps.
   Come, friends, who plough the sea,
    Truce to navigation,
    Take another station;

Let's vary piracee
With a little burglaree!

POLICE (*pianissimo*).   Tarantara, tarantara!

SAM. (*distributing implements to various members of the gang*).
Here's your crowbar and your centrebit,
Your life-preserver—you may want to hit;
Your silent matches, your dark lantern seize,
Take your file and your skeletonic keys.

Enter KING, FREDERIC, *and* RUTH.

ALL (*fortissimo*). With cat-like tread, etc.

RECIT.

FRED.   Hush, hush, not a word! I see a light inside.
The Major-General comes, so quickly hide!

PIRATES.   Yes, yes, the Major-General comes!

[*Exeunt* KING, FREDERIC, SAMUEL, *and* RUTH.

POLICE.   Yes, yes, the Major-General comes!

GEN. (*entering in dressing-gown, carrying a light*).
Yes, yes, the Major-General comes!

SOLO—GENERAL

Tormented with the anguish dread
Of falsehood unatoned,
I lay upon my sleepless bed,
And tossed and turned and groaned.
The man who finds his conscience ache
No peace at all enjoys,
And as I lay in bed awake
I thought I heard a noise.

PIRATES. ⎤   He thought he heard a noise—ha! ha!
POLICE. ⎦   He thought he heard a noise—ha! ha! (*Very loud.*)

GEN.   No, all is still
In dale, on hill;
My mind is set at ease.
So still the scene—
It must have been
The sighing of the breeze.

BALLAD—GENERAL

Sighing softly to the river
  Comes the loving breeze,
Setting nature all a-quiver,
  Rustling through the trees—
ALL.   Through the trees.
GEN. And the brook, in rippling measure,
  Laughs for very love,
While the poplars, in their pleasure,
  Wave their arms above.

POLICE.
and
PIRATES.   Yes, the trees, for very love,
Wave their leafy arms above,
  River, river, little river,
  May thy loving prosper ever.
  Heaven speed thee, poplar tree,
  May thy wooing happy be.

GEN. Yet, the breeze is but a rover;
  When he wings away,
Brook and poplar mourn a lover!
  Sighing well-a-day!
ALL.   Well-a-day!
GEN. Ah! the doing and undoing,
  That the rogue could tell!
When the breeze is out a-wooing,
  Who can woo so well?

POLICE. *and* PIRATES. } Shocking tales the rogue could tell,
Nobody can woo so well.
    Pretty brook, thy dream is over,
    For thy love is but a rover!
    Sad the lot of poplar trees,
    Courted by the fickle breeze!

Enter the GENERAL'S *daughters, all in white peignoirs and night-caps, and carrying lighted candles.*

GIRLS.   Now what is this, and what is that, and why does father leave his rest
At such a time of night as this, so very incompletely dressed?
Dear father is, and always was, the most methodical of men!
It's his invariable rule to go to bed at half-past ten.
What strange occurrence can it be that calls dear father from his rest
At such a time of night as this, so very incompletely dressed?

Enter KING, SAMUEL, *and* FREDERIC.

KING.   Forward, my men, and seize that General there!

(They seize the GENERAL.*)*

GIRLS.   The pirates! the pirates! Oh, despair!
PIRATES.   Yes, we're the pirates, so despair!
GEN.   Frederic here! Oh, joy! Oh, rapture!
Summon your men and effect their capture!
MABEL.   Frederic, save us!
FRED.   Beautiful Mabel,
I would if I could, but I am not able.
PIRATES.   He's telling the truth, he is not able.

KING.   With base deceit
   You worked upon our feelings!
  Revenge is sweet,
   And flavours all our dealings!
  With courage rare
   And resolution manly,
  For death prepare,
   Unhappy General Stanley.

MABEL (*wildly*). Is he to die, unshriven—unannealed?
GIRLS.   Oh, spare him!
MABEL. Will no one in his cause a weapon wield?
GIRLS.   Oh, spare him!
POLICE (*springing up*). Yes, we are here, though hitherto concealed!
GIRLS.   Oh, rapture!
POLICE. So to Constabulary, pirates, yield!
GIRLS.   Oh, rapture!

(*A struggle ensues between Pirates and Police. Eventually the Police are overcome, and fall prostrate, the Pirates standing over them with drawn swords.*)

CHORUS OF POLICE AND PIRATES

You ⎫
We ⎭ triumph now, for well we trow
  Our mortal career's cut short,

No pirate band will take its stand
At the Central Criminal Court.

SERG.   To gain a brief advantage you've contrived,
        But your proud triumph will not be long-lived.

KING.   Don't say you are orphans, for we know that game.

SERG.   On your allegiance we've a stronger claim—
        We charge you yield, in Queen Victoria's name!

KING (*baffled*).   You do!

POLICE.   We do!
        We charge you yield, in Queen Victoria's name!

(*Pirates kneel, Police stand over them triumphantly.*)

KING.   We yield at once, with humbled mien,
        Because, with all our faults, we love our Queen.

POLICE.   Yes, yes, with all their faults, they love their Queen.

GIRLS.   Yes, yes, with all, etc.

(*Police, holding Pirates by the collar, take out handkerchiefs and weep.*)

GEN.   Away with them, and place them at the bar!

Enter RUTH.

RUTH.   One moment! let me tell you who they are.
        They are no members of the common throng;
        They are all noblemen who have gone wrong!

GEN.   No Englishman unmoved that statement hears,
        Because, with all our faults, we love our House of Peers.

RECIT.—GENERAL

I pray you, pardon me, ex-Pirate King,
Peers will be peers, and youth will have its fling.
Resume your ranks and legislative duties,
And take my daughters, all of whom are beauties.

FINALE

Poor wandering ones!
   Though ye have surely strayed,
    Take heart of grace,
    Your steps retrace,
Poor wandering ones!

W. S. GILBERT

Poor wandering ones!
　If such poor love as ours
　Can help you find
　True peace of mind,
Why, take it, it is yours!
　Poor wandering ones! etc.

CURTAIN

The Mikado

OR

THE TOWN OF TITIPU

DRAMATIS PERSONÆ

THE MIKADO OF JAPAN.

NANKI-POO (*his Son, disguised as a wandering minstrel, and in love with* YUM-YUM).

KO-KO (*Lord High Executioner of Titipu*).

POOH-BAH (*Lord High Everything Else*).

PISH-TUSH (*a Noble Lord*).

GO-TO (*a Man of Few Words*).

YUM-YUM
PITTI-SING } *Three Sisters—Wards of* KO-KO.
PEEP-BO

KATISHA (*an elderly Lady, in love with* NANKI-POO).

Chorus of School-girls, Nobles, Guards, and Coolies.

ACT. I.—Courtyard of Ko-Ko's Official Residence.

ACT II.—Ko-Ko's Garden.

First produced at the Savoy Theatre on March 14, 1885.

The Mikado

OR

THE TOWN OF TITIPU

ACT ONE

SCENE.—*Courtyard of* Ko-Ko's *Palace in Titipu.* *Japanese nobles discovered standing and sitting in attitudes suggested by native drawings.*

CHORUS OF NOBLES

If you want to know who we are,
 We are gentlemen of Japan:
On many a vase and jar—
 On many a screen and fan,
  We figure in lively paint:
  Our attitude's queer and quaint—
  You're wrong if you think it ain't, oh!

If you think we are worked by strings,
 Like a Japanese marionette,
You don't understand these things:
 It is simply Court etiquette.
  Perhaps you suppose this throng
  Can't keep it up all day long?
  If that's your idea, you're wrong, oh!

Enter NANKI-POO *in great excitement.* *He carries a native guitar on his back and a bundle of ballads in his hand.*

RECIT.—NANKI-POO

Gentlemen, I pray you tell me
Where a gentle maiden dwelleth,

103

Named Yum-Yum, the ward of Ko-Ko?
In pity speak—oh, speak, I pray you!

A NOBLE. Why, who are you who ask this question?

NANK. Come gather round me, and I'll tell you.

SONG AND CHORUS—NANKI-POO

A wandering minstrel I—
  A thing of shreds and patches,
  Of ballads, songs and snatches,
And dreamy lullaby!

My catalogue is long,
  Through every passion ranging,
  And to your humours changing
I tune my supple song!

Are you in sentimental mood?
  I'll sigh with you,
    Oh, sorrow, sorrow!
On maiden's coldness do you brood?
  I'll do so, too—
    Oh, sorrow, sorrow!
I'll charm your willing ears
With songs of lovers' fears,
While sympathetic tears
  My cheeks bedew—
    Oh, sorrow, sorrow!

But if patriotic sentiment is wanted,
   I've patriotic ballads cut and dried;
For where'er our country's banner may be planted,
   All other local banners are defied!
Our warriors, in serried ranks assembled,
   Never quail—or they conceal it if they do—
And I shouldn't be surprised if nations trembled
   Before the mighty troops of Titipu!

CHORUS.   We shouldn't be surprised, etc.

NANK.   And if you call for a song of the sea,
   We'll heave the capstan round,
With a yo heave ho, for the wind is free,
Her anchor's a-trip and her helm's a-lee,
   Hurrah for the homeward bound!

CHORUS.   Yo-ho—heave ho—
   Hurrah for the homeward bound!

To lay aloft in a howling breeze
   May tickle a landsman's taste,
But the happiest hour a sailor sees
   Is when he's down
   At an inland town,
With his Nancy on his knees, yo ho!
   And his arm around her waist!

CHORUS.   Then man the capstan—off we go,
           As the fiddler swings us round,
        With a yo heave ho,
        And a rumbelow,
           Hurrah for the homeward bound!

A wandering minstrel I, etc.

Enter PISH-TUSH.

PISH.   And what may be your business with Yum-Yum?

NANK.   I'll tell you. A year ago I was a member of the Titipu town band. It was my duty to take the cap round for contributions. While discharging this delicate office, I saw Yum-Yum. We loved each other at once, but she was betrothed to her guardian Ko-Ko, a cheap tailor, and I saw that my suit was hopeless. Overwhelmed with despair, I quitted the town. Judge of my delight when I heard, a month ago, that Ko-Ko had been condemned to death for flirting! I hurried back at once, in the hope of finding Yum-Yum at liberty to listen to my protestations.

PISH.   It is true that Ko-Ko was condemned to death for flirting, but he was reprieved at the last moment, and raised to the exalted rank of Lord High Executioner under the following remarkable circumstances:

SONG—PISH-TUSH *and* CHORUS

Our great Mikado, virtuous man,
When he to rule our land began,

Resolved to try
A plan whereby
 Young men might best be steadied.
So he decreed, in words succinct,
That all who flirted, leered or winked
(Unless connubially linked),
 Should forthwith be beheaded.

  And I expect you'll all agree
  That he was right to so decree.
   And I am right,
   And you are right,
  And all is right as right can be!

CHORUS.   And you are right,
    And we are right, etc.

This stern decree, you'll understand,
Caused great dismay throughout the land!
  For young and old
  And shy and bold
 Were equally affected.
The youth who winked a roving eye,
Or breathed a non-connubial sigh,
Was thereupon condemned to die—
 He usually objected.

  And you'll allow, as I expect,
  That he was right to so object.
   And I am right,
   And you are right,
  And everything is quite correct!

CHORUS.   And you are right,
    And we are right, etc.

And so we straight let out on bail
A convict from the county jail,
  Whose head was next
  On some pretext

Condemnëd to be mown off,
And made *him* Headsman, for we said,
"Who's next to be decapited
Cannot cut off another's head
Until he's cut his own off."

And we are right, I think you'll say,
To argue in this kind of way;
And I am right,
And you are right,
And all is right—too-looral-lay!

CHORUS.　　　　　　　And you are right,
　　　　　　　　　　And we are right, etc.

[*Exeunt* CHORUS.

Enter POOH-BAH.

NANK. Ko-Ko, the cheap tailor, Lord High Executioner of Titipu!
Why, that's the highest rank a citizen can attain!

POOH. It is. Our logical Mikado, seeing no moral difference between
the dignified judge who condemns a criminal to die, and the industrious
mechanic who carries out the sentence, has rolled the two offices into one,
and every judge is now his own executioner.

NANK. But how good of you (for I see that you are a nobleman of
the highest rank) to condescend to tell all this to me, a mere strolling
minstrel!

POOH. Don't mention it. I am, in point of fact, a particularly haughty and exclusive person, of pre-Adamite ancestral descent. You will understand this when I tell you that I can trace my ancestry back to a protoplasmal primordial atomic globule. Consequently, my family pride is something inconceivable. I can't help it. I was born sneering. But I struggle hard to overcome this defect. I mortify my pride continually. When all the great officers of State resigned in a body, because they were too proud to serve under an ex-tailor, did I not unhesitatingly accept all their posts at once?

PISH. And the salaries attached to them? You did.

POOH. It is consequently my degrading duty to serve this upstart as First Lord of the Treasury, Lord Chief Justice, Commander-in-Chief, Lord High Admiral, Master of the Buckhounds, Groom of the Back Stairs, Archbishop of Titipu, and Lord Mayor, both acting and elect, all rolled into one. And at a salary! A Pooh-Bah paid for his services! I a salaried minion! But I do it! It revolts me, but I do it!

NANK. And it does you credit.

POOH. But I don't stop at that. I go and dine with middle-class people on reasonable terms. I dance at cheap suburban parties for a moderate fee. I accept refreshment at any hands, however lowly. I also retail State secrets at a very low figure. For instance, any further information about Yum-Yum would come under the head of a State secret. (NANKI-POO *takes the hint, and gives him money.*) (*Aside.*) Another insult, and, I think, a light one!

SONG—POOH-BAH *with* NANKI-POO *and* PISH-TUSH.

Young man, despair,
　　Likewise go to,
Yum-Yum the fair
　　You must not woo.
　　It will not do:
　　I'm sorry for you,
You very imperfect ablutioner!
　　This very day
　　From school Yum-Yum
Will wend her way,
　　And homeward come,

With beat of drum
And a rum-tum-tum,
To wed the Lord High Executioner!
And the brass will crash,
And the trumpets bray,
And they'll cut a dash
On their wedding day.
She'll toddle away, as all aver,
With the Lord High Executioner!

NANK. *and* POOH.   And the brass will crash, etc.

It's a hopeless case,
As you may see,
And in your place
Away I'd flee;
But don't blame me—
I'm sorry to be
Of your pleasure a diminutioner.
They'll vow their pact
Extremely soon,
In point of fact
This afternoon.
Her honeymoon
With that buffoon
At seven commences, so *you* shun her!

ALL.   And the brass will crash, etc.

[*Exit* PISH-TUSH.

RECIT.—NANKI-POO *and* POOH-BAH

NANK.   And I have journeyed for a month, or nearly,
To learn that Yum-Yum, whom I love so dearly,
This day to Ko-Ko is to be united!
POOH.   The fact appears to be as you've recited:
But here he comes, equipped as suits his station;
He'll give you any further information.

[*Exeunt* POOH-BAH *and* NANKI-POO.

Enter CHORUS OF NOBLES.

Behold the Lord High Executioner!
A personage of noble rank and title—
A dignified and potent officer,
   Whose functions are particularly vital!
      Defer, defer,
To the Lord High Executioner!

Enter KO-KO *attended.*

SOLO—KO-KO

Taken from the county jail
   By a set of curious chances;
Liberated then on bail,
   On my own recognizances;
Wafted by a favouring gale
   As one sometimes is in trances,
To a height that few can scale,
   Save by long and weary dances;
Surely, never had a male
   Under such like circumstances
So adventurous a tale,
   Which may rank with most romances.

CHORUS.   Defer, defer,
To the Lord High Executioner, etc.

KO. Gentlemen, I'm much touched by this reception. I can only trust that by strict attention to duty I shall ensure a continuance of those favours which it will ever be my study to deserve. If I should ever be called upon to act professionally, I am happy to think that there will be no difficulty in finding plenty of people whose loss will be a distinct gain to society at large.

SONG—KO-KO *with* CHORUS OF MEN.

As some day it may happen that a victim must be found,
   I've got a little list—I've got a little list
Of society offenders who might well be underground,

And who never would be missed—who never would be missed!
There's the pestilential nuisances who write for autographs—
All people who have flabby hands and irritating laughs—
All children who are up in dates, and floor you with 'em flat—
All persons who in shaking hands, shake hands with you like *that*—

And all third persons who on spoiling *tête-à-têtes* insist—
  They'd none of 'em be missed—they'd none of 'em be missed.

CHORUS. He's got 'em on the list—he's got 'em on the list;
  And they'll none of 'em be missed—they'll none of 'em be missed.

There's the nigger serenader, and the others of his race,
  And the piano-organist—I've got him on the list!
And the people who eat peppermint and puff it in your face,
  They never would be missed—they never would be missed!
Then the idiot who praises, with enthusiastic tone,
All centuries but this, and every country but his own;
And the lady from the provinces, who dresses like a guy,
And who "doesn't think she waltzes, but would rather like to try";
And that singular anomaly, the lady novelist—
  I don't think she'd be missed—I'm *sure* she'd not be missed!

CHORUS. He's got her on the list—he's got her on the list;
      And I don't think she'll be missed—I'm *sure* she'll not be missed!

And that *Nisi Prius* nuisance, who just now is rather rife,
  The Judicial humorist—I've got *him* on the list!
All funny fellows, comic men, and clowns of private life—
  They'd none of 'em be missed—they'd none of 'em be missed!
And apologetic statesmen of a compromising kind,
Such as—What d'ye call him—Thing'em-bob, and likewise—Never-mind,
And 'St—'st—'st—and What's-his-name, and also You-know-who—
The task of filling up the blanks I'd rather leave to *you*.
But it really doesn't matter whom you put upon the list,
  For they'd none of 'em be missed—they'd none of 'em be missed!

CHORUS. You may put 'em on the list—you may put 'em on the list;
      And they'll none of 'em be missed—they'll none of 'em be missed!

Enter POOH-BAH.

KO. Pooh-Bah, it seems that the festivities in connection with my approaching marriage must last a week. I should like to do it handsomely, and I want to consult you as to the amount I ought to spend upon them.

POOH. Certainly. In which of my capacities? As First Lord of the Treasury, Lord Chamberlain, Attorney-General, Chancellor of the Exchequer, Privy Purse, or Private Secretary?

KO. Suppose we say as Private Secretary.

POOH. Speaking as your Private Secretary, I should say that, as the city will have to pay for it, don't stint yourself, do it well.

KO. Exactly—as the city will have to pay for it. That is your advice.

POOH. As Private Secretary. Of course you will understand that, as Chancellor of the Exchequer, I am bound to see that due economy is observed.

KO. Oh! But you said just now "Don't stint yourself, do it well."

POOH. As Private Secretary.

KO. And now you say that due economy must be observed.

POOH. As Chancellor of the Exchequer.

KO. I see. Come over here, where the Chancellor can't hear us. (*They cross the stage.*) Now, as my Solicitor, how do you advise me to deal with this difficulty?

POOH. Oh, as your Solicitor, I should have no hesitation in saying "Chance it——"

KO. Thank you. (*Shaking his hand.*) I will.

POOH. If it were not that, as Lord Chief Justice, I am bound to see that the law isn't violated.

KO. I see. Come over here where the Chief Justice can't hear us. (*They cross the stage.*) Now, then, as First Lord of the Treasury?

POOH. Of course, as First Lord of the Treasury, I could propose a special vote that would cover all expenses, if it were not that, as Leader of the Opposition, it would be my duty to resist it, tooth and nail. Or, as Paymaster-General, I could so cook the accounts that, as Lord High Auditor, I should never discover the fraud. But then, as Archbishop of Titipu, it would be my duty to denounce my dishonesty and give myself into my own custody as First Commissioner of Police.

KO. That's extremely awkward.

POOH. I don't say that all these distinguished people couldn't be squared; but it is right to tell you that they wouldn't be sufficiently degraded in their own estimation unless they were insulted with a very considerable bribe.

KO. The matter shall have my careful consideration. But my bride and her sisters approach, and any little compliment on your part, such as an abject grovel in a characteristic Japanese attitude, would be esteemed a favour.   *[Exeunt together.*

Enter procession of YUM-YUM's *schoolfellows, heralding* YUM-YUM, PEEP-BO, *and* PITTI-SING.

CHORUS OF GIRLS

Comes a train of little ladies
   From scholastic trammels free,
Each a little bit afraid is,
   Wondering what the world can be!

Is it but a world of trouble—
   Sadness set to song?
Is its beauty but a bubble
   Bound to break ere long?

Are its palaces and pleasures
   Fantasies that fade?

115

And the glory of its treasures
  Shadow of a shade?

Schoolgirls we, eighteen and under,
  From scholastic trammels free,
And we wonder—how we wonder!—
  What on earth the world can be!

TRIO

YUM-YUM, PEEP-BO, *and* PITTI-SING, *with* CHORUS OF GIRLS.

THE THREE.   Three little maids from school are we,
              Pert as a school-girl well can be,
              Filled to the brim with girlish glee,
                  Three little maids from school!
YUM-YUM.   Everything is a source of fun. (*Chuckle.*)
PEEP-BO.   Nobody's safe, for we care for none! (*Chuckle.*)
PITTI-SING.   Life is a joke that's just begun! (*Chuckle.*)
THE THREE.   Three little maids from school!
ALL (*dancing*). Three little maids who, all unwary,
              Come from a ladies' seminary,
              Freed from its genius tutelary—
THE THREE (*suddenly demure*).
                  Three little maids from school!

YUM-YUM.   One little maid is a bride, Yum-Yum—
PEEP-BO.   Two little maids in attendance come—
PITTI-SING.   Three little maids is the total sum.
THE THREE.   Three little maids from school!
YUM-YUM.   From three little maids take one away.
PEEP-BO.   Two little maids remain, and they—
PITTI-SING.   Won't have to wait very long, they say—
THE THREE.   Three little maids from school!
ALL (*dancing*). Three little maids who, all unwary,
              Come from a ladies' seminary,
              Freed from its genius tutelary—
THE THREE (*suddenly demure*).
                  Three little maids from school!

116

Enter KO-KO *and* POOH-BAH.

KO. At last, my bride that is to be! (*About to embrace her.*)

YUM. You're not going to kiss me before all these people?

KO. Well, that was the idea.

YUM (*aside to Peep-Bo*). It seems odd, doesn't it?

PEEP. It's rather peculiar.

PITTI. Oh, I expect it's all right. Must have a beginning, you know.

YUM. Well, of course I know nothing about these things; but I've no objection if it's usual.

KO. Oh, it's quite usual, I think. Eh, Lord Chamberlain? (*Appealing to* POOH-BAH.)

POOH. I have known it done. (KO-KO *embraces her.*)

YUM. Thank goodness that's over! (*Sees* NANKI-POO, *and rushes to him.*) Why, that's never you? (*The Three Girls rush to him and shake his hands, all speaking at once.*)

> YUM. Oh, I'm so glad! I haven't seen you for ever so long, and I'm right at the top of the school, and I've got three prizes, and I've come home for good, and I'm not going back any more!
>
> PEEP. And have you got an engagement?—Yum-Yum's got one, but she doesn't like it, and she'd ever so much rather it was you! I've come home for good, and I'm not going back any more!
>
> PITTI. Now tell us all the news, because you go about everywhere, and we've been at school, but, thank goodness, that's all over now, and we've come home for good, and we're not going back any more!

(*These three speeches are spoken together in one breath.*)

KO. I beg your pardon. Will you present me?

YUM. } Oh, this is the musician who used—

PEEP. } Oh, this is the gentleman who used—

PITTI. } Oh, it is only Nanki-Poo who used—

KO. One at a time, if you please.

YUM. Oh, if you please he's the gentleman who used to play so beautifully on the—on the——

PITTI. On the Marine Parade.

YUM. Yes, I think that was the name of the instrument.

NANK. Sir, I have the misfortune to love your ward, Yum-Yum—oh, I know I deserve your anger!

KO. Anger! not a bit, my boy. Why, I love her myself. Charming little girl, isn't she? Pretty eyes, nice hair. Taking little thing, altogether. Very glad to hear my opinion backed by a competent authority. Thank you very much. Good-bye. (*To* PISH-TUSH.) Take him away. (PISH-TUSH *removes him.*)

PITTI (*who has been examining* POOH-BAH). I beg your pardon, but what is this? Customer come to try on?

KO. That is a Tremendous Swell.

PITTI. Oh, it's alive. (*She starts back in alarm.*)

POOH. Go away, little girls. Can't talk to little girls like you. Go away, there's dears.

KO. Allow me to present you, Pooh-Bah. These are my three wards. The one in the middle is my bride elect.

POOH. What do you want me to do to them? Mind, I *will not* kiss them.

KO. No, no, you shan't kiss them; a little bow—a mere nothing—, you needn't mean it, you know.

POOH. It goes against the grain. They are not young ladies, they are young persons.

KO. Come, come, make an effort, there's a good nobleman.

POOH. (*aside to* KO-KO). Well, I shan't mean it. (*With a great effort.*) How de do, little girls, how de do? (*Aside.*) Oh, my protoplasmal ancestor!

KO. That's very good. (*Girls indulge in suppressed laughter.*)

POOH. I see nothing to laugh at. It is very painful to me to have to say "How de do, little girls, how de do?" to young persons. I'm not in the habit of saying "How de do, little girls, how de do?" to anybody under the rank of a Stockbroker.

KO. (*aside to girls*). Don't laugh at him, he can't help it—he's under treatment for it. (*Aside to* POOH-BAH.) Never mind them, they don't understand the delicacy of your position.

POOH. We know how delicate it is, don't we?

KO. I should think we did! How a nobleman of your importance can do it at all is a thing I never can, never shall understand.

[KO-KO *retires up and goes off.*

QUARTET AND CHORUS OF GIRLS.

YUM-YUM, PEEP-BO, PITTI-SING, *and* POOH-BAH.

YUM., PEEP. and PITTI.
So please you, Sir, we much regret
If we have failed in etiquette
Towards a man of rank so high—
We shall know better by and by.

YUM.
But youth, of course, must have its fling,
So pardon us,
So pardon us,

PITTI.
And don't, in girlhood's happy spring,
Be hard on us,
Be hard on us,
If we're inclined to dance and sing.
Tra la la, etc. (*Dancing.*)

CHORUS OF GIRLS. But youth, of course, etc.

POOH.
I think you ought to recollect
You cannot show too much respect
Towards the highly titled few;
But nobody does, and why should you?
That youth at us should have its fling,
Is hard on us,
Is hard on us;
To our prerogative we cling—
So pardon us,
So pardon us,
If we decline to dance and sing.
Tra la la, etc. (*Dancing.*)

CHORUS OF GIRLS. But youth, of course, must have its fling, etc.

[*Exeunt all but* YUM-YUM.

Enter NANKI-POO.

NANK. Yum-Yum, at last we are alone! I have sought you night and day for three weeks, in the belief that your guardian was beheaded, and I find that you are about to be married to him this afternoon!

YUM. Alas, yes!

NANK. But you do not love him?

YUM. Alas, no!

NANK. Modified rapture! But why do you not refuse him?

YUM. What good would that do? He's my guardian, and he wouldn't let me marry you!

NANK. But I would wait until you were of age!

YUM. You forget that in Japan girls do not arrive at years of discretion until they are fifty.

NANK. True; from seventeen to forty-nine are considered years of indiscretion.

YUM. Besides—a wandering minstrel, who plays a wind instrument outside tea-houses, is hardly a fitting husband for the ward of a Lord High Executioner.

NANK. But—— (*Aside.*) Shall I tell her? Yes! She will not betray me! (*Aloud.*) What if it should prove that, after all, I am no musician?

YUM. There! I was certain of it, directly I heard you play!

NANK. What if it should prove that I am no other than the son of his Majesty the Mikado?

YUM. The son of the Mikado! But why is your Highness disguised? And what has your Highness done? And will your Highness promise never to do it again?

NANK. Some years ago I had the misfortune to captivate Katisha, an elderly lady of my father's Court. She misconstrued my customary affability into expressions of affection, and claimed me in marriage, under my father's law. My father, the Lucius Junius Brutus of his race, ordered me to marry her within a week, or perish ignominiously on the scaffold. That night I fled his Court, and, assuming the disguise of a Second Trombone, I joined the band in which you found me when I had the happiness of seeing you! (*Approaching her.*)

YUM (*retreating*). If you please, I think your Highness had better not come too near. The laws against flirting are excessively severe.

NANK. But we are quite alone, and nobody can see us.

YUM. Still, that doesn't make it right. To flirt is capital.

NANK. It *is* capital!

YUM. And we must obey the law.

NANK. Deuce take the law!

YUM. I wish it would, but it won't!

NANK. If it were not for that, how happy we might be!

YUM. Happy indeed!

NANK. If it were not for the law, we should now be sitting side by side, like that. (*Sits by her.*)

YUM. Instead of being obliged to sit half a mile off, like that. (*Crosses and sits at other side of stage.*)

NANK. We should be gazing into each other's eyes, like that. (*Gazing at her sentimentally.*)

YUM. Breathing sighs of unutterable love—like that. (*Sighing and gazing lovingly at him.*)

NANK. With our arms round each other's waists, like that. (*Embracing her.*)

YUM. Yes, if it wasn't for the law.

NANK. If it wasn't for the law.

YUM. As it is, of course we couldn't do anything of the kind.

NANK. Not for worlds!

YUM. Being engaged to Ko-Ko, you know!

NANK. Being engaged to Ko-Ko!

DUET—YUM-YUM *and* NANKI-POO

NANK.
Were you not to Ko-Ko plighted,
    I would say in tender tone,
"Loved one, let us be united—
    Let us be each other's own!"
I would merge all rank and station,
    Worldly sneers are nought to us,
And, to mark my admiration,
    I would kiss you fondly thus—   (*Kisses her.*)

BOTH.
I / He } would kiss { you / me } fondly thus—   (*Kiss.*)

YUM.
But as I'm engaged to Ko-Ko,
To embrace you thus, *con fuoco*,
Would distinctly be no *giuoco*,
And for yam I should get toko—

121

BOTH. Toko, toko, toko, toko!

NANK. So, in spite of all temptation,
    Such a theme I'll not discuss,
And on no consideration
    Will I kiss you fondly thus—   (*Kissing her.*)
Let me make it clear to you,
This is what I'll never do!
    This, oh, this, oh, this, oh, this—   (*Kissing her.*)

TOGETHER. This, oh, this, etc.

        [*Exeunt in opposite directions.*

Enter KO-KO.

KO. (*looking after* YUM-YUM). There she goes! To think how entirely my future happiness is wrapped up in that little parcel! Really, it hardly seems worth while! Oh, matrimony!— (*Enter* POOH-BAH *and* PISH-TUSH.) Now then, what is it? Can't you see I'm soliloquizing? You have interrupted an apostrophe, sir!

PISH. I am the bearer of a letter from his Majesty the Mikado.

KO. (*taking it from him reverentially*). A letter from the Mikado! What in the world can he have to say to me? (*Reads letter.*) Ah, here it is at last! I thought it would come sooner or later! The Mikado is struck by the fact that no executions have taken place in Titipu for a year, and decrees that unless somebody is beheaded within one month the post of Lord High Executioner shall be abolished, and the city reduced to the rank of a village!

PISH. But that will involve us all in irretrievable ruin!

KO. Yes. There is no help for it, I shall have to execute somebody at once. The only question is, who shall it be?

POOH. Well, it seems unkind to say so, but as you're already under sentence of death for flirting, everything seems to point to *you*.

KO. To me? What are you talking about? I can't execute myself.

POOH. Why not?

KO. Why not? Because, in the first place, self-decapitation is an extremely difficult, not to say dangerous, thing to attempt; and, in the second, it's suicide, and suicide is a capital offence.

POOH. That is so, no doubt.

PISH. We might reserve that point.

POOH. True, it could be argued six months hence, before the full Court.

KO. Besides, I don't see how a man *can* cut off his own head.

POOH. A man might try.

PISH. Even if you only succeeded in cutting it half off, that would be something.

POOH. It would be taken as an earnest of your desire to comply with the Imperial will.

KO. No. Pardon me, but there I am adamant. As official Headsman, my reputation is at stake, and I can't consent to embark on a professional operation unless I see my way to a successful result.

POOH. This professional conscientiousness is highly creditable to *you*, but it places us in a very awkward position.

KO. My good sir, the awkwardness of your position is grace itself compared with that of a man engaged in the act of cutting off his own head.

PISH. I am afraid that, unless you can obtain a substitute——

KO. A substitute? Oh, certainly—nothing easier. (*To* POOH-BAH.) Pooh-Bah, I appoint you Lord High Substitute.

POOH. I should be delighted. Such an appointment would realize my fondest dreams. But no, at any sacrifice, I must set bounds to my insatiable ambition!

TRIO

Ko-Ko	POOH-BAH	PISH-TUSH
My brain it teems	I am so proud,	I heard one day
With endless schemes	If I allowed	A gentleman say
Both good and new	My family pride	That criminals who
For Titipu;	To be my guide,	Are cut in two
But if I flit,	I'd volunteer	Can hardly feel
The benefit	To quit this sphere	The fatal steel,
That I'd diffuse	Instead of you,	And so are slain
The town would lose!	In a minute or two.	Without much pain.
Now every man	But family pride	If this is true,
To aid his clan	Must be denied,	It's jolly for you;
Should plot and plan	And set aside,	Your courage screw

TRIO (*Continued*)

Ko-Ko	Pooh-Bah	Pish-Tush
As best he can,	And mortified.	To bid us adieu,
And so,	And so,	And go
Although	Although	And show
I'm ready to go,	I wish to go,	Both friend and foe
Yet recollect	And greatly pine	How much you dare.
'Twere disrespect	To brightly shine,	I'm quite aware
Did I neglect	And take the line	It's your affair,
To thus effect	Of a hero fine,	Yet I declare
This aim direct,	With grief condign	I'd take your share,
So I object—	I must decline—	But I don't much care—
So I object—	I must decline—	I don't much care—
So I object—	I must decline—	I don't much care—

ALL.   To sit in solemn silence in a dull, dark dock,
In a pestilential prison, with a life-long lock,
Awaiting the sensation of a short, sharp shock,
From a cheap and chippy chopper on a big black block!

                              [*Exeunt* POOH. *and* PISH.

KO. This is simply appalling! I, who allowed myself to be respited at the last moment, simply in order to benefit my native town, am now required to die within a month, and that by a man whom I have loaded with honours! Is this public gratitude? Is this—— (*Enter* NANKI-POO, *with a rope in his hands.*) Go away, sir! How dare you? Am I never to be permitted to soliloquize?

NANK. Oh, go on—don't mind me.

KO. What are you going to do with that rope?

NANK. I am about to terminate an unendurable existence.

KO. Terminate your existence? Oh, nonsense! What for?

NANK. Because you are going to marry the girl I adore.

KO. Nonsense, sir. I won't permit it. I am a humane man, and if you attempt anything of the kind I shall order your instant arrest. Come, sir, desist at once or I summon my guard.

NANK. That's absurd. If you attempt to raise an alarm, I instantly perform the Happy Despatch with this dagger.

KO. No, no, don't do that. This is horrible! (*Suddenly.*) Why, you cold-blooded scoundrel, are you aware that, in taking your life, you are committing a crime which—which—which is—— Oh! (*Struck by an idea.*) Substitute!

NANK. What's the matter?

KO. Is it *absolutely certain* that you are resolved to die?

NANK. Absolutely!

KO. Will *nothing* shake your resolution?

NANK. Nothing.

KO. Threats, entreaties, prayers—all useless?

NANK. All! My mind is made up.

KO. Then, if you really mean what you say, and if you are absolutely resolved to die, and if nothing whatever will shake your determination—don't spoil yourself by committing suicide, but be beheaded handsomely at the hands of the Public Executioner!

NANK. I don't see how that would benefit me.

KO. You don't? Observe: you'll have a month to live, and you'll live like a fighting-cock at my expense. When the day comes there'll be a grand public ceremonial—you'll be the central figure—no one will attempt to deprive you of that distinction. There'll be a procession—bands—dead march—bells tolling—all the girls in tears—Yum-Yum distracted—then, when it's all over, general rejoicings, and a display of fireworks in the evening. *You* won't see them, but they'll be there all the same.

NANK. Do you think Yum-Yum would really be distracted at my death?

KO. I am convinced of it. Bless you, she's the most tender-hearted little creature alive.

NANK. I should be sorry to cause her pain. Perhaps, after all, if I were to withdraw from Japan, and travel in Europe for a couple of years, I might contrive to forget her.

KO. Oh, I don't think you could forget Yum-Yum so easily; and, after all, what is more miserable than a love-blighted life?

NANK. True.

KO. Life without Yum-Yum—why, it seems absurd!

NANK. And yet there are a good many people in the world who have to endure it.

KO. Poor devils, yes! You are quite right not to be of their number.

NANK. (*suddenly*). I *won't* be of their number!

KO. Noble fellow!

NANK. I'll tell you how we'll manage it. Let me marry Yum-Yum to-morrow, and in a month you may behead me.

KO. No, no. I draw the line at Yum-Yum.

NANK. Very good. If you can draw the line, so can I. (*Preparing rope.*)

KO. Stop, stop—listen one moment—be reasonable. How can I consent to your marrying Yum-Yum if I'm going to marry her myself?

NANK. My good friend, she'll be a widow in a month, and you can marry her then.

KO. That's true, of course. I quite see that. But, dear me! my position during the next month will be most unpleasant—most unpleasant.

NANK. Not half so unpleasant as my position at the end of it.

KO. But—dear me!—well—I agree—after all, it's only putting off my wedding for a month. But you won't prejudice her against me, will you? You see, I've educated her to be my wife; she's been taught to regard me as a wise and good man. Now I shouldn't like her views on that point disturbed.

NANK. Trust me, she shall never learn the truth from me.

FINALE

Enter CHORUS, POOH-BAH, *and* PISH-TUSH.

CHORUS

With aspect stern
 And gloomy stride,
We come to learn
 How you decide.

Don't hesitate
 Your choice to name,
A dreadful fate
 You'll suffer all the same.

POOH. To ask you what you mean to do we punctually appear.
KO. Congratulate me, gentlemen, I've found a Volunteer!
ALL. The Japanese equivalent for Hear, Hear, Hear!

KO. (*presenting him*).   'Tis Nanki-Poo!
ALL.   Hail, Nanki-Poo!
KO.   I think he'll do?
ALL.   Yes, yes, he'll do!
KO. He yields his life if I'll Yum-Yum surrender.
    Now I adore that girl with passion tender,
    And could not yield her with a ready will,
        Or her allot,
        If I did not
    Adore myself with passion tenderer still!

Enter YUM-YUM, PEEP-BO, *and* PITTI-SING.

ALL.   Ah, yes!
    He loves himself with passion tenderer still!
KO. (*to* NANKI-POO).   Take her—she's yours!

              [*Exit* KO-KO.

ENSEMBLE

NANKI-POO.   The threatened cloud has passed away,
YUM-YUM.   And brightly shines the dawning day;
NANKI-POO.   What though the night may come too soon,
YUM-YUM.   There's yet a month of afternoon!

NANKI-POO, POOH-BAH, YUM-YUM, PITTI-SING, *and* PEEP-BO.

    Then let the throng
    Our joy advance,
    With laughing song
    And merry dance,

CHORUS.   With joyous shout and ringing cheer,
    Inaugurate our brief career!

PITTI-SING.   A day, a week, a month, a year——
YUM.   Or far or near, or far or near,

POOH.   Life's eventime comes much too soon,
PITTI-SING.   You'll live at least a honeymoon!

ALL.   Then let the throng, etc.

CHORUS.   With joyous shout, etc.

SOLO—POOH-BAH

As in a month you've got to die,
    If Ko-Ko tells us true,
'Twere empty compliment to cry
    "Long life to Nanki-Poo!"
But as one month you have to live
    As fellow-citizen,
This toast with three times three we'll give—
    "Long life to you—till then!"

                [*Exit* POOH-BAH.

CHORUS.   May all good fortune prosper you,
             May you have health and riches too,
             May you succeed in all you do!
             Long life to you—till then!

(*Dance.*)

Enter KATISHA *melodramatically.*

KAT.   Your revels cease! Assist me, all of you!
CHORUS.   Why, who is this whose evil eyes
          Rain blight on our festivities?
KAT.   I claim my perjured lover, Nanki-Poo!
          Oh, fool! to shun delights that never cloy!
CHORUS.   Go, leave thy deadly work undone!
KAT.   Come back, oh, shallow fool! come back to joy!
CHORUS.   Away, away! ill-favoured one!
NANK. (*aside to* YUM-YUM). Ah!
          'Tis Katisha!
          The maid of whom I told you. (*About to go.*)

KAT. (*detaining him*). No!
>> You shall not go,
>> These arms shall thus enfold you!

SONG—KATISHA

KAT. (*addressing* NANKI-POO).
>> Oh fool, that fleest
>>> My hallowed joys!
>> Oh blind, that seest
>>> No equipoise!
>> Oh rash, that judgest
>>> From half, the whole!
>> Oh base, that grudgest
>>> Love's lightest dole!
>>> Thy heart unbind,
>>> Oh fool, oh blind!
>>> Give me my place,
>>> Oh rash, oh base!

CHORUS.
>> If she's thy bride, restore her place,
>> Oh fool, oh blind, oh rash, oh base!

KAT. (*addressing* YUM-YUM).
>> Pink cheek, that rulest
>>> Where wisdom serves!
>> Bright eye, that foolest
>>> Heroic nerves!
>> Rose lip, that scornest
>>> Lore-laden years!
>> Smooth tongue, that warnest
>>> Who rightly hears!
>>> Thy doom is nigh,
>>> Pink cheek, bright eye!
>>> Thy knell is rung,
>>> Rose lip, smooth tongue!

CHORUS.
>> If true her tale, thy knell is rung,
>> Pink cheek, bright eye, rose lip, smooth tongue!

129

PITTI-SING. Away, nor prosecute your quest—
From our intention, well expressed,
 You cannot turn us!
The state of your connubial views
Towards the person you accuse
 Does not concern us!
For he's going to marry Yum-Yum—

ALL.   Yum-Yum!

PITTI.   Your anger pray bury,
   For all will be merry,
I think you had better succumb—

ALL.   Cumb—cumb!

PITTI. And join our expressions of glee.
On this subject I pray you be dumb—

ALL.   Dumb—dumb.

PITTI.   You'll find there are many
   Who'll wed for a penny—
The word for your guidance is "Mum"—

ALL.   Mum—mum!

PITTI. There's lots of good fish in the sea!

ALL. On this subject we pray you be dumb, etc.

SOLO—KATISHA

The hour of gladness
 Is dead and gone;
In silent sadness
 I live alone!
The hope I cherished
 All lifeless lies,
And all has perished
 Save love, which never dies!
Oh, faithless one, this insult you shall rue!
In vain for mercy on your knees you'll sue.
I'll tear the mask from your disguising!

NANK. (*aside*).   Now comes the blow!
KAT. Prepare yourselves for new surprising!
NANK. (*aside*).   How foil my foe?
KAT. No minstrel he, despite bravado!

YUM. (*aside, struck by an idea*).   Ha! ha! I know!

KAT.   He is the son of your——

(NANKI-POO, YUM-YUM, *and* CHORUS, *interrupting, sing Japanese words, to drown her voice.*)

                    O ni! bikkuri shakkuri to!

KAT.   In vain you interrupt with this tornado!
                He is the only son of your——

ALL.   O ni! bikkuri shakkuri to!

KAT.   I'll spoil——

ALL.   O ni! bikkuri shakkuri to!

KAT.   Your gay gambado!
                He is the son——

ALL.   O ni! bikkuri shakkuri to!

KAT.   Of your——

ALL.   O ni! bikkuri shakkuri to!

KAT.   The son of your——

ALL.   O ni! bikkuri shakkuri to! oya! oya!

ENSEMBLE

KATISHA	THE OTHERS
Ye torrents roar!	We'll hear no more,
Ye tempests howl!	Ill-omened owl,
Your wrath outpour	To joy we soar,
With angry growl!	Despite your scowl!
Do ye your worst, my vengeance call	The echoes of our festival
Shall rise triumphant over all!	Shall rise triumphant over all!
Prepare for woe,	Away you go,
Ye haughty lords,	Collect your hordes;
At once I go	Proclaim your woe
Mikado-wards,	In dismal chords;
My wrongs with vengeance shall be crowned!	We do not heed their dismal sound,
My wrongs with vengeance shall be crowned!	For joy reigns everywhere around.

(KATISHA *rushes furiously up stage, clearing the crowd away right and left, finishing on steps at the back of stage.*)

END OF ACT I

ACT TWO

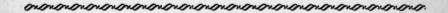

SCENE.—KO-KO's *Garden.*

YUM-YUM *discovered seated at her bridal toilet, surrounded by maidens, who are dressing her hair and painting her face and lips, as she judges of the effect in a mirror.*

SOLO—PITTI-SING *and* CHORUS OF GIRLS

CHORUS.
> Braid the raven hair—
> Weave the supple tress—
> Deck the maiden fair
> In her loveliness—
> Paint the pretty face—
> Dye the coral lip—
> Emphasize the grace
> Of her ladyship!
> Art and nature, thus allied,
> Go to make a pretty bride.

THE MIKADO

SOLO—PITTI-SING

Sit with downcast eye—
    Let it brim with dew—
Try if you can cry—
    We will do so, too.
When you're summoned, start
    Like a frightened roe—
Flutter, little heart,
    Colour, come and go!
Modesty at marriage-tide
Well becomes a pretty bride!

CHORUS

Braid the raven hair, etc.

[*Exeunt* PITTI-SING, PEEP-BO, *and* CHORUS.

YUM. Yes, I am indeed beautiful! Sometimes I sit and wonder, in my artless Japanese way, why it is that I am so much more attractive than anybody else in the whole world. Can this be vanity? No! Nature is lovely and rejoices in her loveliness. I am a child of Nature, and take after my mother.

SONG—YUM-YUM

The sun, whose rays
Are all ablaze
    With ever-living glory,
Does not deny
His majesty—
    He scorns to tell a story!
He don't exclaim,
    "I blush for shame,
    So kindly be indulgent."
But, fierce and bold,
In fiery gold,
    He glories all effulgent!

    I mean to rule the earth,
        As he the sky—

133

We really know our worth,
   The sun and I!

Observe his flame,
That placid dame,
  The moon's Celestial Highness;
There's not a trace
Upon her face

  Of diffidence or shyness:
She borrows light
That, through the night,
  Mankind may all acclaim her!
And, truth to tell,
She lights up well,
  So I, for one, don't blame her!

Ah, pray make no mistake,
We are not shy;
We're very wide awake,
The moon and I!

Enter PITTI-SING *and* PEEP-BO.

YUM. Yes, everything seems to smile upon me. I am to be married to-day to the man I love best, and I believe I am the very happiest girl in Japan!

PEEP. The happiest girl indeed, for she is indeed to be envied who has attained happiness in all but perfection.

YUM. In "all but" perfection?

PEEP. Well, dear, it can't be denied that the fact that your husband is to be beheaded in a month is, in its way, a drawback. It does seem to take the top off it, you know.

PITTI. I don't know about that. It all depends!

PEEP. At all events, *he* will find it a drawback.

PITTI. Not necessarily. Bless you, it all depends!

YUM. (*in tears*). I think it very indelicate of you to refer to such a subject on such a day. If my married happiness *is* to be—to be——

PEEP. Cut short.

YUM. Well, cut short—in a month, can't you let me forget it? (*Weeping.*)

Enter NANKI-POO, *followed by* GO-TO.

NANK. Yum-Yum in tears—and on her wedding morn!

YUM. (*sobbing*). They've been reminding me that in a month you're to be beheaded! (*Bursts into tears.*)

PITTI. Yes, we've been reminding her that you're to be beheaded. (*Bursts into tears.*)

PEEP. It's quite true, you know, you *are* to be beheaded! (*Bursts into tears.*)

NANK. (*aside*). Humph! Now, some bridegrooms would be depressed by this sort of thing! (*Aloud.*) A month? Well, what's a month? Bah! These divisions of time are purely arbitrary. Who says twenty-four hours make a day?

PITTI. There's a popular impression to that effect.

NANK. Then we'll efface it. We'll call each second a minute—each minute an hour—each hour a day—and each day a year. At that rate we've about thirty years of married happiness before us!

PEEP. And, at that rate, this interview has already lasted four hours and three-quarters!

[*Exit* PEEP-BO.

YUM. (*still sobbing*). Yes. How time flies when one is thoroughly enjoying oneself!

NANK. That's the way to look at it! Don't let's be downhearted! There's a silver lining to every cloud.

YUM. Certainly. Let's—let's be perfectly happy! (*Almost in tears.*)

GO-TO. By all means. Let's—let's thoroughly enjoy ourselves.

PITTI. It's—it's absurd to cry! (*Trying to force a laugh.*)

YUM. Quite ridiculous! (*Trying to laugh.*)

(*All break into a forced and melancholy laugh.*)

MADRIGAL

YUM-YUM, PITTI-SING, NANKI-POO, *and* PISH-TUSH.

Brightly dawns our wedding day;
　　Joyous hour, we give thee greeting!
　　Whither, whither art thou fleeting?
Fickle moment, prithee stay!
　　What though mortal joys be hollow?
　　Pleasures come, if sorrows follow:
Though the tocsin sound, ere long,
　　Ding dong! Ding dong!
Yet until the shadows fall
Over one and over all,
Sing a merry madrigal—
　　　　A madrigal!
Fal-la—fal-la! etc. (*Ending in tears.*)

Let us dry the ready tear,
　　Though the hours are surely creeping
　　Little need for woeful weeping,

Till the sad sundown is near.
All must sip the cup of sorrow—
I to-day and thou to-morrow;
This the close of every song—
Ding dong! Ding dong!
What, though solemn shadows fall,
Sooner, later, over all?
Sing a merry madrigal—
A madrigal!
Fal-la—fal-la! etc. (*Ending in tears.*)

[*Exeunt* PITTI-SING *and* PISH-TUSH.

(NANKI-POO *embraces* YUM-YUM. *Enter* KO-KO. NANKI-POO *releases* YUM-YUM.)

KO. Go on—don't mind me.

NANK. I'm afraid we're distressing you.

KO. Never mind, I must get used to it. Only please do it by degrees. Begin by putting your arm round her waist. (NANKI-POO *does so.*) There; let me get used to that first.

YUM. Oh, wouldn't you like to retire? It must pain you to see us so affectionate together!

KO. No, I must learn to bear it! Now oblige me by allowing her head to rest on your shoulder.

NANK. Like that? (*He does so.* KO-KO *much affected.*)

KO. I am much obliged to you. Now—kiss her! (*He does so.* KO-KO *writhes with anguish.*) Thank you—it's simple torture!

YUM. Come, come, bear up. After all, it's only for a month.

KO. No. It's no use deluding oneself with false hopes.

NANK. ⎫
YUM.   ⎬ What do you mean?

KO. (*to* YUM-YUM). My child—my poor child! (*Aside.*) How shall I break it to her? (*Aloud.*) My little bride that was to have been——

YUM. (*delighted*). *Was to have been?*

KO. Yes, you never can be mine!

NANK. ⎫   ⎧What!
YUM. ⎬ (*in ecstasy*). ⎨I'm so glad!

137

KO. I've just ascertained that, by the Mikado's law, when a married man is beheaded his wife is buried alive.

NANK. ⎫
      ⎬ Buried alive!
YUM. ⎭

KO. Buried alive. It's a most unpleasant death.

NANK. But whom did you get that from?

KO. Oh, from Pooh-Bah. He's my Solicitor.

YUM. But he may be mistaken!

KO. So I thought; so I consulted the Attorney-General, the Lord Chief Justice, the Master of the Rolls, the Judge Ordinary, and the Lord Chancellor. They're all of the same opinion. Never knew such unanimity on a point of law in my life!

NANK. But stop a bit! This law has never been put in force.

KO. Not yet. You see, flirting is the only crime punishable with decapitation, and married men never flirt.

NANK. Of course, they don't. I quite forgot that! Well, I suppose I may take it that my dream of happiness is at an end!

YUM. Darling—I don't want to appear selfish, and I love you with all my heart—I don't suppose I shall ever love anybody else half as much —but when I agreed to marry you—my own—I had no idea—pet—that I should have to be buried alive in a month!

NANK. Nor I! It's the very first I've heard of it!

YUM. It—it makes a difference, doesn't it?

NANK. It *does* make a difference, of course.

YUM. You see—burial alive—it's such a stuffy death!

NANK. I call it a beast of a death.

YUM. You see my difficulty, don't you?

NANK. Yes, and I see my own. If I insist on your carrying out your promise, I doom you to a hideous death; if I release you, you marry Ko-Ko at once!

TRIO—YUM-YUM, NANKI-POO, and KO-KO.

YUM.   Here's a how-de-do!
       If I marry you,
     When your time has come to perish,
     Then the maiden whom you cherish

138

Must be slaughtered, too!
Here's a how-de-do!

NANK.   Here's a pretty mess!
In a month, or less,
I must die without a wedding!
Let the bitter tears I'm shedding
Witness my distress,
Here's a pretty mess!

KO.   Here's a state of things!
To her life she clings!
Matrimonial devotion
Doesn't seem to suit her notion—
Burial it brings!
Here's a state of things!

ENSEMBLE

YUM-YUM *and* NANKI POO	KO-KO
With a passion that's intense	With a passion that's intense
I worship and adore,	You worship and adore,
But the laws of common sense	But the laws of common sense
We oughtn't to ignore.	You oughtn't to ignore.
If what he says is true,	If what I say is true,
'Tis death to marry you!	'Tis death to marry you!
Here's a pretty state of things!	Here's a pretty state of things!
Here's a pretty how-de-do!	Here's a pretty how-de-do!

[*Exit* YUM-YUM.

KO. (*going up to* NANKI-POO). My poor boy, I'm really very sorry for you.

NANK. Thanks, old fellow. I'm sure you are.

KO. You see I'm quite helpless.

NANK. I quite see that.

KO. I can't conceive anything more distressing than to have one's marriage broken off at the last moment. But you shan't be disappointed of a wedding—you shall come to mine.

NANK. It's awfully kind of you, but that's impossible.

KO. Why so?

NANK. To-day I die.

KO. What do you mean?

NANK. I can't live without Yum-Yum. This afternoon I perform the Happy Despatch.

KO. No, no—pardon me—I can't allow that.

NANK. Why not?

KO. Why, hang it all, you're under contract to die by the hand of the Public Executioner in a month's time! If you kill yourself, what's to become of me? Why, I shall have to be executed in your place!

NANK. It would certainly seem so!

Enter POOH-BAH.

KO. Now then, Lord Mayor, what is it?

POOH. The Mikado and his suite are approaching the city, and will be here in ten minutes.

KO. The Mikado! He's coming to see whether his orders have been carried out! (*To* NANKI-POO.) Now look here, you know—this is getting serious—a bargain's a bargain, and you really mustn't frustrate the ends of justice by committing suicide. As a man of honour and a gentleman, you are bound to die ignominiously by the hands of the Public Executioner.

NANK. Very well, then—behead me.

KO. What, now?

NANK. Certainly; at once.

POOH. Chop it off! Chop it off!

KO. My good sir, I don't go about prepared to execute gentlemen at a moment's notice. Why, I never even killed a blue-bottle!

POOH. Still, as Lord High Executioner——

KO. My good sir, as Lord High Executioner, I've got to behead him in a month. I'm not ready yet. I don't know how it's done. I'm going to take lessons. I mean to begin with a guinea pig, and work my way through the animal kingdom till I come to a Second Trombone. Why, you don't suppose that, as a humane man, I'd have accepted the post of Lord High Executioner if I hadn't thought the duties were purely nominal? I *can't* kill you—I can't kill anything! I can't kill anybody! (*Weeps.*)

NANK. Come, my poor fellow, we all have unpleasant duties to discharge at times; after all, what is it? If I don't mind, why should you? Remember, sooner or later it must be done.

KO. (*springing up suddenly*). *Must it?* I'm not so sure about that!

NANK. What do you mean?

KO. Why should I kill you when making an affidavit that you've been executed will do just as well? Here are plenty of witnesses—the Lord Chief Justice, Lord High Admiral, Commander-in-Chief, Secretary of State for the Home Department, First Lord of the Treasury, and Chief Commissioner of Police.

NANK. But where are they?

KO. There they are. They'll all swear to it—won't you? (*To* POOH-BAH.)

POOH. Am I to understand that all of us high Officers of State are required to perjure ourselves to ensure your safety?

KO. Why not? You'll be grossly insulted, as usual.

POOH. Will the insult be cash down, or at a date?

KO. It will be a ready-money transaction.

POOH. (*Aside.*) Well, it will be a useful discipline. (*Aloud.*) Very good. Choose your fiction, and I'll endorse it! (*Aside.*) Ha! ha! Family Pride, how do you like *that,* my buck?

NANK. But I tell you that life without Yum-Yum——

KO. Oh, Yum-Yum, Yum-Yum! Bother Yum-Yum! Here, Commissionaire (*to* POOH-BAH), go and fetch Yum-Yum. (*Exit* POOH-BAH.) Take Yum-Yum and marry Yum-Yum, only go away and never come back again. (*Enter* POOH-BAH *with* YUM-YUM.) Here she is. Yum-Yum, are you particularly busy?

YUM. Not particularly.

KO. You've five minutes to spare?

YUM. Yes.

KO. Then go along with his Grace the Archbishop of Titipu; he'll marry you at once.

YUM. But if I'm to be buried alive?

KO. Now, don't ask any questions, but do as I tell you, and Nanki-Poo will explain all.

NANK. But one moment——

KO. Not for worlds. Here comes the Mikado, no doubt to ascertain whether I've obeyed his decree, and if he finds you alive I shall have the greatest difficulty in persuading him that I've beheaded you. (*Exeunt* NANKI-POO *and* YUM-YUM, *followed by* POOH-BAH.) Close thing that, for here he comes!

[*Exit* KO-KO.

March.—Enter procession, heralding MIKADO, *with* KATISHA.

Entrance of MIKADO *and* KATISHA.

("March of the Mikado's troops.")

CHORUS.
> Miya sama, miya sama,
> On n'm-ma no mayé ni
> Pira-Pira suru no wa
> Nan gia na
> Toko tonyaré tonyaré na?

DUET—MIKADO *and* KATISHA

MIK.
> From every kind of man
> Obedience I expect;
> I'm the Emperor of Japan—

KAT.
> And I'm his daughter-in-law elect!
> He'll marry his son
> (He's only got one)
> To his daughter-in-law elect.

MIK.   My morals have been declared
  Particularly correct;

KAT.   But they're nothing at all, compared
  With those of his daughter-in-law elect!
   Bow—Bow—
  To his daughter-in-law elect!

ALL.   Bow—Bow—
  To his daughter-in-law elect!

MIK.   In a fatherly kind of way
  I govern each tribe and sect,
 All cheerfully own my sway—

KAT.   Except his daughter-in-law elect!
  As tough as a bone,
  With a will of her own,
 Is his daughter-in-law elect!

MIK.   My nature is love and light—
  My freedom from all defect—

KAT.   Is insignificant quite,
  Compared with his daughter-in-law elect!
   Bow—Bow—
  To his daughter-in-law elect!

ALL.   Bow—Bow—
  To his daughter-in-law elect!

SONG—MIKADO *and* CHORUS

A more humane Mikado never
 Did in Japan exist,
  To nobody second,
  I'm certainly reckoned
 A true philanthropist.
It is my very humane endeavour
 To make, to some extent,
  Each evil liver

A running river
Of harmless merriment.

My object all sublime
I shall achieve in time—
To let the punishment fit the crime—
    The punishment fit the crime;
And make each prisoner pent
Unwillingly represent
A source of innocent merriment!
Of innocent merriment!

All prosy dull society sinners,
    Who chatter and bleat and bore,
        Are sent to hear sermons
        From mystical Germans
    Who preach from ten till four.
The amateur tenor, whose vocal villainies
    All desire to shirk,
        Shall, during off-hours,
        Exhibit his powers
    To Madame Tussaud's waxwork.

The lady who dies a chemical yellow,
    Or stains her grey hair puce,
        Or pinches her figger,
        Is blacked like a nigger
    With permanent walnut juice.
The idiot who, in railway carriages,
    Scribbles on window-panes,
        We only suffer
        To ride on a buffer
    In Parliamentary trains.

My object all sublime, etc.

CHORUS.   His object all sublime, etc.

The advertising quack who wearies
    With tales of countless cures,

His teeth, I've enacted,
Shall all be extracted
By terrified amateurs.

The music-hall singer attends a series
  Of masses and fugues and "ops"
    By Bach, interwoven
    With Spohr and Beethoven,
At classical Monday Pops.

The billiard sharp whom any one catches,
  His doom's extremely hard—
    He's made to dwell—
    In a dungeon cell
On a spot that's always barred.
And there he plays extravagant matches
  In fitless finger-stalls
    On a cloth untrue,
    With a twisted cue
And elliptical billiard balls!

     My object all sublime, etc.

CHORUS.   His object all sublime, etc.

W. S. GILBERT

Enter POOH-BAH, KO-KO, *and* PITTI-SING. *All kneel.*

(POOH-BAH *hands a paper to* KO-KO.)

KO. I am honoured in being permitted to welcome your Majesty. I guess the object of your Majesty's visit—your wishes have been attended to. The execution has taken place.

MIK. Oh, you've had an execution, have you?

KO. Yes. The Coroner has just handed me his certificate.

POOH. I am the Coroner. (KO-KO *hands certificate to* MIKADO.)

MIK. And this is the certificate of his death. (*Reads.*) "At Titipu, in the presence of the Lord Chancellor, Lord Chief Justice, Attorney-General, Secretary of State for the Home Department, Lord Mayor, and Groom of the Second Floor Front——"

POOH. They were all present, your Majesty. I counted them myself.

MIK. Very good house. I wish I'd been in time for the performance.

KO. A tough fellow he was, too—a man of gigantic strength. His struggles were terrific. It was really a remarkable scene.

MIK. Describe it.

TRIO *and* CHORUS

KO-KO, PITTI-SING, POOH-BAH *and* CHORUS.

KO.
The criminal cried, as he dropped him down,
In a state of wild alarm—
With a frightful, frantic, fearful frown,
I bared my big right arm.
I seized him by his little pig-tail,
And on his knees fell he,
As he squirmed and struggled,
And gurgled and guggled,
I drew my snickersnee!
Oh, never shall I
Forget the cry,
Or the shriek that shriekèd he,
As I gnashed my teeth,
When from its sheath
I drew my snickersnee!

146

CHORUS

We know him well,
He cannot tell
Untrue or groundless tales—
He always tries
To utter lies,
And every time he fails.

PITTI.

He shivered and shook as he gave the sign
  For the stroke he didn't deserve;
When all of a sudden his eye met mine,
  And it seemed to brace his nerve;
For he nodded his head and kissed his hand,
  And he whistled an air, did he,
    As the sabre true
    Cut cleanly through
His cervical vertebræ!
    When a man's afraid,
    A beautiful maid
Is a cheering sight to see;
    And it's oh, I'm glad
    That moment sad
Was soothed by sight of me!

CHORUS

Her terrible tale
You can't assail,
With truth it quite agrees:
Her taste exact
For faultless fact
Amounts to a disease.

POOH.

Now though you'd have said that head was dead
  (For its owner dead was he),
It stood on its neck, with a smile well-bred,
  And bowed three times to me!
It was none of your impudent off-hand nods,
  But as humble as could be;

For it clearly knew
The deference due
To a man of pedigree!
And it's oh, I vow,
This deathly bow
Was a touching sight to see;
Though trunkless, yet
It couldn't forget
The deference due to me!

CHORUS

This haughty youth,
He speaks the truth
Whenever he finds it pays:
And in this case
It all took place
Exactly as he says!

[*Exeunt* CHORUS.

MIK. All this is very interesting, and I should like to have seen it. But we came about a totally different matter. A year ago my son, the heir to the throne of Japan, bolted from our Imperial Court.

KO. Indeed! Had he any reason to be dissatisfied with his position?

KAT. None whatever. On the contrary, I was going to marry him—yet he fled!

POOH. I am surprised that he should have fled from one so lovely!

KAT. That's not true.

POOH. No!

KAT. You hold that I am not beautiful because my face is plain. But you know nothing; you are still unenlightened. Learn, then, that it is not in the face alone that beauty is to be sought. My face is unattractive!

POOH. It is.

KAT. But I have a left shoulder-blade that is a miracle of loveliness. People come miles to see it. My right elbow has a fascination that few can resist.

POOH. Allow me!

KAT. It is on view Tuesdays and Fridays, on presentation of visiting card. As for my circulation, it is the largest in the world.

KO. And yet he fled!

MIK. And is now masquerading in this town, disguised as a Second Trombone.

KO.
POOH. } A Second Trombone!
PITTI.

MIK. Yes; would it be troubling you too much if I asked you to produce him? He goes by the name of——

KAT. Nanki-Poo.

MIK. Nanki-Poo.

KO. It's quite easy. That is, it's rather difficult. In point of fact, he's gone abroad!

MIK. Gone abroad! His address.

KO. Knightsbridge!

KAT. (*who is reading certificate of death*). Ha!

MIK. What's the matter?

KAT. See here—his name—Nanki-Poo—beheaded this morning. Oh, where shall I find another? Where shall I find another?

(KO-KO, POOH-BAH, *and* PITTI-SING *fall on their knees.*)

MIK. (*looking at paper*). Dear, dear, dear! this is very tiresome. (*To* KO-KO.) My poor fellow, in your anxiety to carry out my wishes you have beheaded the heir to the throne of Japan!

KO. I beg to offer an unqualified apology.

POOH. I desire to associate myself with that expression of regret.

PITTI. We really hadn't the least notion——

MIK. Of course you hadn't. How could you? Come, come, my good fellow, don't distress yourself—it was no fault of yours. If a man of exalted rank chooses to disguise himself as a Second Trombone, he must take the consequences. It really distresses me to see you take on so. I've no doubt he thoroughly deserved all he got. (*They rise.*)

KO. We are infinitely obliged to your Majesty——

PITTI. Much obliged, your Majesty.

POOH. Very much obliged, your Majesty.

MIK. Obliged? not a bit. Don't mention it. How *could* you tell?

POOH. No, of course we couldn't tell who the gentleman really was.

PITTI. It wasn't written on his forehead, you know.

KO. It might have been on his pocket-handkerchief, but Japanese don't use pocket-handkerchiefs! Ha! ha! ha!

MIK. Ha! ha! ha! (*To* KATISHA.) I forget the punishment for compassing the death of the Heir Apparent.

KO., POOH., *and* PITTI. Punishment. (*They drop down on their knees again.*)

MIK. Yes. Something lingering, with boiling oil in it, I fancy. Something of that sort. I think boiling oil occurs in it, but I'm not sure. I know it's something humorous, but lingering, with either boiling oil or melted lead. Come, come, don't fret—I'm not a bit angry.

KO. (*in abject terror*). If your Majesty will accept our assurance, we had no idea——

MIK. Of course——

PITTI. I knew nothing about it.

POOH. I wasn't there.

MIK. That's the pathetic part of it. Unfortunately, the fool of an Act says "compassing the death of the Heir Apparent." There's not a word about a mistake——

KO., PITTI., *and* POOH. No!

MIK. Or not knowing——

KO. No!

MIK. Or having no notion——

PITTI. No!

MIK. Or not being there——

POOH. No!

MIK. There should be, of course——

KO., PITTI., *and* POOH. Yes!

MIK. But there isn't.

KO., PITTI., *and* POOH. Oh!

MIK. That's the slovenly way in which these Acts are always drawn. However, cheer up, it'll be all right. I'll have it altered next session. Now, let's see about your execution—will after luncheon suit you? Can you wait till then?

KO., PITTI., *and* POOH. Oh, yes—we can wait till then!

MIK. Then we'll make it after luncheon.

POOH. I don't want any lunch.

MIK. I'm really very sorry for you all, but it s an unjust world, and virtue is triumphant only in theatrical performances.

GLEE

PITTI-SING, KATISHA, KO-KO, POOH-BAH, *and* MIKADO.

MIK.   See how the Fates their gifts allot,
For A is happy—B is not.
Yet B is worthy, I dare say,
Of more prosperity than A!

KO., POOH., *and* PITTI. *Is* B more worthy?

KAT.   I should say
He's worth a great deal more than A.

ENSEMBLE.   Yet A is happy!
Oh, so happy!
Laughing, Ha! ha!
Chaffing, Ha! ha!
Nectar quaffing, Ha! ha! ha!
Ever joyous, ever gay,
Happy, undeserving A!

KO., POOH., *and* PITTI.
If I were Fortune—which I'm not—
B should enjoy A's happy lot,
And A should die in miserie—
That is, assuming I am B.

MIK. *and* KAT.   But *should* A perish?

KO., POOH., *and* PITTI.   That should he
(Of course, assuming I am B).
B should be happy!
Oh, so happy!
Laughing, Ha! ha!
Chaffing, Ha! ha!
Nectar quaffing, Ha! ha! ha!
But condemned to die is he,
Wretched meritorious B!

                     [*Exeunt* MIKADO *and* KATISHA.

KO. Well, a nice mess you've got us into, with your nodding head and the deference due to a man of pedigree!

POOH. Merely corroborative detail, intended to give artistic verisimilitude to an otherwise bald and unconvincing narrative.

PITTI. Corroborative detail indeed! Corroborative fiddlestick!

KO. And you're just as bad as he is with your cock-and-a-bull stories about catching his eye and his whistling an air. But that's so like you! You must put in your oar!

POOH. But how about your big right arm?

PITTI. Yes, and your snickersnee!

KO. Well, well, never mind that now. There's only one thing to be done. Nanki-Poo hasn't started yet—he must come to life again at once. (*Enter* NANKI-POO *and* YUM-YUM *prepared for journey.*) Here he comes. Here, Nanki-Poo, I've good news for you—you're reprieved.

NANK. Oh, but it's too late. I'm a dead man, and I'm off for my honeymoon.

KO. Nonsense! A terrible thing has just happened. It seems you're the son of the Mikado.

NANK. Yes, but that happened some time ago.

KO. Is this a time for airy persiflage? Your father is here, and with Katisha!

NANK. My father! And with Katisha!

KO. Yes, he wants you particularly.

POOH. So does she.

YUM. Oh, but he's married now.

KO. But, bless my heart! what has that to do with it?

NANK. Katisha claims me in marriage, but I can't marry her because I'm married already—consequently she will insist on my execution, and if I'm executed, my wife will have to be buried alive.

YUM. You see our difficulty.

KO. Yes. I don't know what's to be done.

NANK. There's one chance for you. If you could persuade Katisha to marry you, she would have no further claim on me, and in that case I could come to life without any fear of being put to death.

KO. I marry Katisha!

YUM. I really think it's the only course.

KO. But, my good girl, have you seen her? She's something appalling!

PITTI. Ah! that's only her face. She has a left elbow which people come miles to see!

POOH. I am told that her right heel is much admired by connoisseurs.

KO. My good sir, I decline to pin my heart upon any lady's right heel.

NANK. It comes to this: While Katisha is single, I prefer to be a disembodied spirit. When Katisha is married, existence will be as welcome as the flowers in spring.

DUET—NANKI-POO *and* KOKO

(*With* YUM-YUM, PITTI-SING, *and* POOH-BAH.)

NANK. The flowers that bloom in the spring,
Tra la,
Breathe promise of merry sunshine—
As we merrily dance and we sing
Tra la,
We welcome the hope that they bring,
Tra la,
Of a summer of roses and wine.
And that's what we mean when we say that a thing
Is welcome as flowers that bloom in the spring.
Tra la la la la la la, etc.

ALL. Tra la la la, etc.

KO. The flowers that bloom in the spring,
Tra la,
Have nothing to do with the case.
I've got to take under my wing,
Tra la,
A most unattractive old thing,
Tra la,
With a caricature of a face.
And that's what I mean when I say, or I sing,
"Oh, bother the flowers that bloom in the spring."
Tra la la la la la, etc.

153

ALL.   Tra la la la, Tra la la la, etc.

[*Dance and exeunt* NANKI-POO, YUM-YUM,
POOH-BAH, PITTI-SING, *and* KO-KO.

Enter KATISHA.

RECITATIVE AND SONG—KATISHA

Alone, and yet alive! Oh, sepulchre!
My soul is still my body's prisoner!
Remote the peace that Death alone can give—
My doom, to wait! my punishment, to live!

SONG

Hearts do not break!
They sting and ache
For old love's sake,
    But do not die,
Though with each breath
They long for death
As witnesseth
    The living I!
        Oh, living I!
        Come, tell me why,
        When hope is gone,
        Dost thou stay on?
        Why linger here,
        Where all is drear?
        Oh, living I!
        Come, tell me why,
        When hope is gone,
        Dost thou stay on?
    May not a cheated maiden die?

KO. (*entering and approaching her timidly*). Katisha!
KAT. The miscreant who robbed me of my love! But vengeance
pursues—they are heating the cauldron!
KO. Katisha—behold a suppliant at your feet! Katisha—mercy!

KAT. Mercy? Had you mercy on him? See here, you! You have slain my love. He did not love *me,* but he would have loved me in time. I am an acquired taste—only the educated palate can appreciate *me.* I was educating *his* palate when he left me. Well, he is dead, and where shall I find another? It takes years to train a man to love me. Am I to go through the weary round again, and, at the same time, implore mercy for you who robbed me of my prey—I mean my pupil—just as his education was on the point of completion? Oh, where shall I find another?

KO. (*suddenly, and with great vehemence*). Here!— Here!

KAT. What!!!

KO. (*with intense passion*). Katisha, for years I have loved you with a white-hot passion that is slowly but surely consuming my very vitals! Ah, shrink not from me! If there is aught of woman's mercy in your heart, turn not away from a love-sick suppliant whose every fibre thrills at your tiniest touch! True it is that, under a poor mask of disgust, I have endeavoured to conceal a passion whose inner fires are broiling the soul within me! But the fire will not be smothered—it defies all attempts at extinction, and, breaking forth, all the more eagerly for its long restraint, it declares itself in words that will not be weighed—that cannot be schooled—that should not be too severely criticised. Katisha, I dare not hope for your love—but I will not live without it! Darling!

KAT. You, whose hands still reek with the blood of my betrothed, dare to address words of passion to the woman you have so foully wronged!

KO. I do—accept my love, or I perish on the spot!

KAT. Go to! Who knows so well as I that no one ever yet died of a broken heart!

KO. You know not what you say. Listen!

SONG—KO-KO

On a tree by a river a little tom-tit
    Sang "Willow, titwillow, titwillow!"
And I said to him, "Dicky-bird, why do you sit
    Singing 'Willow, titwillow, titwillow'?"
"Is it weakness of intellect, birdie?" I cried,

"Or a rather tough worm in your little inside?"
With a shake of his poor little head, he replied,
    "Oh, willow, titwillow, titwillow!"

He slapped at his chest, as he sat on that bough
    Singing "Willow, titwillow, titwillow!"
And a cold perspiration bespangled his brow,
    "Oh, willow, titwillow, titwillow!"
He sobbed and he sighed, and a gurgle he gave,
Then he plunged himself into the billowy wave,
And an echo arose from the suicide's grave—
    "Oh, willow, titwillow, titwillow!"

Now I feel just as sure as I'm sure that my name
    Isn't Willow, titwillow, titwillow,
That 'twas blighted affection that made him exclaim,
    "Oh, willow, titwillow, titwillow!"
And if you remain callous and obdurate, I
Shall perish as he did, and you will know why,
Though I probably shall not exclaim as I die,
    "Oh, willow, titwillow, titwillow!"

(During this song KATISHA *has been greatly affected, and
at the end is almost in tears.)*

KAT. *(whimpering).* Did he really die of love?

KO. He really did.

KAT. All on account of a cruel little hen?

KO. Yes.

KAT. Poor little chap!

KO. It's an affecting tale, and quite true. I knew the bird intimately.

KAT. Did you? He must have been very fond of her.

KO. His devotion was something extraordinary.

KAT. *(still whimpering).* Poor little chap! And—and if I refuse you,
will you go and do the same?

KO. At once.

KAT. No, no—you mustn't! Anything but that! *(Falls on his breast.)*
Oh, I'm a silly little goose!

KO. *(making a wry face).* You are!

KAT. And you won't hate me because I'm just a little teeny weeny
wee bit bloodthirsty, will you?

KO. Hate you? Oh, Katisha! is there not beauty even in blood-
thirstiness?

KAT. My idea exactly.

DUET—KATISHA *and* KO-KO

KAT. There is beauty in the bellow of the blast,
There is grandeur in the growling of the gale,
There is eloquent outpouring
When the lion is a-roaring,
And the tiger is a-lashing of his tail!

KO. Yes, I like to see a tiger
From the Congo or the Niger,
And especially when lashing of his tail!

KAT. Volcanoes have a splendour that is grim,
And earthquakes only terrify the dolts,
But to him who's scientific
There's nothing that's terrific
In the falling of a flight of thunderbolts!

KO. Yes, in spite of all my meekness,
If I have a little weakness,
It's a passion for a flight of thunderbolts!

BOTH. If that is so,
Sing derry down derry!
It's evident, very,
Our tastes are one.
Away we'll go,
And merrily marry,
Nor tardily tarry
Till day is done!

KO. There is beauty in extreme old age—
Do you fancy you are elderly enough?
Information I'm requesting
On a subject interesting:
Is a maiden all the better when she's tough?

KAT. Throughout this wide dominion
It's the general opinion
That she'll last a good deal longer when she's tough.

KO. Are you old enough to marry, do you think?
Won't you wait till you are eighty in the shade?
There's a fascination frantic
In a ruin that's romantic;
Do you think you are sufficiently decayed?

KAT.   To the matter that you mention
           I have given some attention,
       And I think I am sufficiently decayed.
BOTH.   If that is so,
             Sing derry down derry!
             It's evident, very,
               Our tastes are one!
         Away we'll go,
           And merrily marry,
           Nor tardily tarry
             Till day is done!

[Exeunt together.

Flourish. Enter the MIKADO, *attended by* PISH-TUSH *and Court.*

MIK. Now then, we've had a capital lunch, and we're quite ready. Have all the painful preparations been made?

PISH. Your Majesty, all is prepared.

MIK. Then produce the unfortunate gentleman and his two well-meaning but misguided accomplices.

Enter KO-KO, KATISHA, POOH-BAH, *and* PITTI-SING.
They throw themselves at the MIKADO'S *feet.*

KAT. Mercy! Mercy for Ko-Ko! Mercy for Pitti-Sing! Mercy even for Pooh-Bah!

MIK. I beg your pardon, I don't think I quite caught that remark.

POOH. Mercy even for Pooh-Bah.

KAT. Mercy! My husband that was to have been is dead, and I have just married this miserable object.

MIK. Oh! You've not been long about it!

KO. We were married before the Registrar.

POOH. *I* am the Registrar.

MIK. I see. But my difficulty is that, as you have slain the Heir Apparent——

Enter NANKI-POO *and* YUM-YUM. *They kneel.*

NANKI. The Heir Apparent is *not* slain.

MIK. Bless my heart, my son!

159

YUM. And your daughter-in-law elected!

KAT. (*seizing* KO-KO). Traitor, you have deceived me!

MIK. Yes, you are entitled to a little explanation, but I think he will give it better whole than in pieces.

KO. Your Majesty, it's like this: It is true that I stated that I had killed Nanki-Poo——

MIK. Yes, with most affecting particulars.

POOH. Merely corroborative detail intended to give artistic verisimilitude to a bald and——

KO. *Will* you refrain from putting in your oar? (*To* MIKADO.) It's like this: When your Majesty says, "Let a thing be done," it's as good as done—practically, it *is* done—because your Majesty's will is law. Your Majesty says, "Kill a gentleman," and a gentleman is told off to be killed. Consequently, that gentleman is as good as dead—practically, he *is* dead—and if he is dead, why not say so?

MIK. I see. Nothing could possibly be more satisfactory!

FINALE

PITTI.	For he's gone and married Yum-Yum—
ALL.	Yum-Yum!
PITTI.	Your anger pray bury,
	For all will be merry,
	I think you had better succumb—
ALL.	Cumb—cumb!
PITTI.	And join our expressions of glee!
KO.	On this subject I pray you be dumb—
ALL.	Dumb—dumb!
KO.	Your notions, though many,
	Are not worth a penny,
	The word for your guidance is "Mum"—
ALL.	Mum—Mum!
KO.	You've a very good bargain in me.
ALL.	On this subject we pray you be dumb—
	Dumb—dumb!
	We think you had better succumb—
	Cumb—cumb!

You'll find there are many
Who'll wed for a penny,
There are lots of good fish in the sea.

YUM. *and* NANK. The threatened cloud has passed away,
And brightly shines the dawning day;
What though the night may come too soon,
We've years and years of afternoon!

ALL. Then let the throng
Our joy advance,
With laughing song
And merry dance,
With joyous shout and ringing cheer,
Inaugurate our new career!
Then let the throng, etc.

CURTAIN

The Bab

Ballads

GENERAL JOHN

THE bravest names for fire and flames
And all that mortal durst,
Were GENERAL JOHN and PRIVATE JAMES,
Of the Sixty-seventy-first.

GENERAL JOHN was a soldier tried,
A chief of warlike dons;
A haughty stride and a withering pride
Were MAJOR-GENERAL JOHN's.

A sneer would play on his martial phiz,
  Superior birth to show;
"Pish!" was a favourite word of his,
  And he often said "Ho! ho!"

Full-Private James described might be,
  As a man of a mournful mind;
No characteristic trait had he
  Of any distinctive kind.

From the ranks, one day, cried Private James,
  "Oh! Major-General John,
I've doubts of our respective names,
  My mournful mind upon.

"A glimmering thought occurs to me
  (Its source I can't unearth),
But I've a kind of a notion we
  Were cruelly changed at birth.

"I've a strange idea that each other's names
  We've each of us here got on.
Such things have been," said Private James.
  "They have!" sneered General John.

GENERAL JOHN

"My General John, I swear upon
  My oath I think 'tis so——"
"Pish!" proudly sneered his General John,
  And he also said "Ho! ho!"

"My General John! my General John!
  My General John!" quoth he,
"This aristocratical sneer upon
  Your face I blush to see!

"No truly great or generous cove
  Deserving of them names,
Would sneer at a fixed idea that's drove
  In the mind of a Private James!"

Said General John, "Upon your claims
  No need your breath to waste;
If this is a joke, Full-Private James,
  It's a joke of doubtful taste.

"But, being a man of doubtless worth,
  If you feel certain quite
That we were probably changed at birth,
  I'll venture to say you're right."

167

So General John as Private James
  Fell in, parade upon;
And Private James, by change of names,
  Was Major-General John.

TO A LITTLE MAID

BY A POLICEMAN

Come with me, little maid!
Nay, shrink not, thus afraid—
        I'll harm thee not!
Fly not, my love, from me—
I have a home for thee—
        A fairy grot,
            Where mortal eye
            Can rarely pry,
There shall thy dwelling be!

List to me, while I tell
The pleasures of that cell,
        Oh, little maid!
What though its couch be rude—
Homely the only food
        Within its shade?
            No thought of care
            Can enter there,
No vulgar swain intrude!

169

W. S. GILBERT

Come with me, little maid,
Come to the rocky shade
   I love to sing;
Live with us, maiden rare—
Come, for we "want" thee there,
  Thou elfin thing,
    To work thy spell,
    In some cool cell
In stately Pentonville!

SIR GUY THE CRUSADER

Sir Guy was a doughty crusader,
  A muscular knight,
  Ever ready to fight,
A very determined invader,
  And Dickey de Lion's delight.

Lenore was a Saracen maiden,
  Brunette, statuesque,
  The reverse of grotesque,
Her pa was a bagman from Aden,
  Her mother she played in burlesque.

A *coryphée*, pretty and loyal,
  In amber and red
  The ballet she led;
Her mother performed at the Royal,
  Lenore at the Saracen's Head.

Of face and of figure majestic,
  She dazzled the cits—
  Ecstaticised pits;—
Her troubles were only domestic,
  But drove her half out of her wits.

Her father incessantly lashed her,
 On water and bread
 She was grudgingly fed;
Whenever her father he thrashed her
 Her mother sat down on her head.

Guy saw her, and loved her, with reason,
 For beauty so bright
 Sent him mad with delight;
He purchased a stall for the season,
 And sat in it every night.

His views were exceedingly proper,
 He wanted to wed,
 So he called at her shed
And saw her progenitor whop her—
 Her mother sit down on her head.

"So pretty," said he, "and so trusting!
 You brute of a dad,
 You unprincipled cad,
Your conduct is really disgusting,
 Come, come, now admit it's too bad!

"You're a turbaned old Turk, and malignant—
 Your daughter Lenore
 I intensely adore,

And I cannot help feeling indignant,
  A fact that I hinted before;

"To see a fond father employing
    A deuce of a knout
    For to bang her about,
To a sensitive lover's annoying."
  Said the bagman, "Crusader, get out."

Says Guy, "Shall a warrior laden
    With a big spiky knob,
    Sit in peace on his cob
While a beautiful Saracen maiden
  Is whipped by a Saracen snob?

"To London I'll go from my charmer."
    Which he did, with his loot
    (Seven hats and a flute),
And was nabbed for his Sydenham armour
  At Mr. Ben-Samuel's suit.

Sir Guy he was lodged in the Compter,
    Her pa, in a rage,
    Died (don't know his age),
His daughter, she married the prompter,
  Grew bulky and quitted the stage.

HAUNTED

HAUNTED? Ay, in a social way,
By a body of ghosts in a dread array:
But no conventional spectres they—
    Appalling, grim, and tricky:
I quail at mine as I'd never quail
At a fine traditional spectre pale,
With a turnip head and a ghostly wail,
    And a splash of blood on the dicky!

Mine are horrible social ghosts,
Speeches and women and guests and hosts,
Weddings and morning calls and toasts,
    In every bad variety:
Ghosts that hover about the grave
Of all that's manly, free, and brave:
You'll find their names on the architrave
    Of that charnel-house, Society.

Black Monday—black as its school-room ink—
With its dismal boys that snivel and think
Of its nauseous messes to eat and drink,
    And its frozen tank to wash in.

HAUNTED

That was the first that brought me grief,
And made me weep, till I sought relief
In an emblematical handkerchief,
    To choke such baby bosh in.

First and worst in the grim array—
Ghosts of ghosts that have gone their way,
Which I wouldn't revive for a single day
    For all the wealth of PLUTUS—
Are the horrible ghosts that school-days scared:
If the classical ghost that BRUTUS dared
Was the ghost of his "Cæsar" unprepared,
    I'm sure I pity BRUTUS.

I pass to critical seventeen;
The ghost of that terrible wedding scene,
When an elderly Colonel stole my Queen,
    And woke my dream of heaven.
No schoolgirl decked in her nurse-room curls
Was my gushing innocent Queen of Pearls;
If she wasn't a girl of a thousand girls,
    She was one of forty-seven!

I see the ghost of my first cigar,
Of the thence-arising family jar—
Of my maiden brief (I was at the Bar,
    And I called the Judge "Your wushup!")
Of reckless days and reckless nights,
With wrenched-off knockers, extinguished lights,
Unholy songs and tipsy fights,
    Which I strove in vain to hush up.

Ghosts of fraudulent joint-stock banks,
Ghosts of "copy, declined with thanks,"
Of novels returned in endless ranks,
    And thousands more, I suffer.
The only line to fitly grace
My humble tomb, when I've run my race,
Is, "Reader, this is the resting-place
    Of an unsuccessful duffer."

I've fought them all, these ghosts of mine,
But the weapons I've used are sighs and brine,
And now that I'm nearly forty-nine,
    Old age is my chiefest bogy;
For my hair is thinning away at the crown,
And the silver fights with the worn-out brown;
And a general verdict sets me down
    As an irreclaimable fogy.

LORENZO DE LARDY

Dalilah de Dardy adored
  The very correctest of cards,
Lorenzo de Lardy, a lord—
  He was one of Her Majesty's Guards.

Dalilah de Dardy was fat,
  Dalilah de Dardy was old—
(No doubt in the world about that)
  But Dalilah de Dardy had gold.

Lorenzo de Lardy was tall,
  The flower of maidenly pets,
Young ladies would love at his call,
  But Lorenzo de Lardy had debts.

His money-position was queer,
  And one of his favourite freaks
Was to hide himself, three times a year,
  In Paris, for several weeks.

Many days didn't pass him before
  He fanned himself into a flame,
For a beautiful "Dam du Comptwore,"
  And this was her singular name:

W. S. GILBERT

Alice Eulalie Coraline
 Euphrosine Colombina Thérèse
Juliette Stephanie Celestine
 Charlotte Russe de la Sauce Mayonnaise.

She booked all the orders and tin,
 Accoutred in showy fal-lal,
At a two-fifty Restaurant, in
 The glittering Palais Royal.

He'd gaze in her orbit of blue,
 Her hand he would tenderly squeeze,
But the words of her tongue that he knew
 Were limited strictly to these:

"Coraline Celestine Eulalie,
 Houp là! Je vous aime, oui, mossoo,
Combien donnez moi aujourd'hui
 Bonjour, Mademoiselle, parlez voo."

Mademoiselle de la Sauce Mayonnaise
 Was a witty and beautiful miss,
Extremely correct in her ways,
 But her English consisted of this:

LORENZO DE LARDY

"Oh my! pretty man, if you please,
 Blom boodin, biftek, currie lamb,
Bouldogue, two franc half, quite ze cheese,
 Rosbif, me spik Angleesh, godam."

A waiter, for seasons before,
 Had basked in her beautiful gaze,
And burnt to dismember Milor,
 He loved DE LA SAUCE MAYONNAISE.

He said to her, "Méchante THÉRÈSE,
 Avec désespoir tu m'accables.
Penses-tu, DE LA SAUCE MAYONNAISE,
 Ses intentions sont honorables?

"Flirtez toujours, ma belle, si tu ôses—
 Je me vengerai ainsi, ma chère,
Je lui dirai de quoi l'on compose
 Vol au vent à la Financière!"

LORD LARDY knew nothing of this—
 The waiter's devotion ignored,
But he gazed on the beautiful miss,
 And never seemed weary or bored.

179

The waiter would screw up his nerve,
  His fingers he'd snap and he'd dance—
And LORD LARDY would smile and observe,
  "How strange are the customs of France!"

Well, after delaying a space,
  His tradesmen no longer would wait:
Returning to England apace,
  He yielded himself to his fate.

LORD LARDY espoused, with a groan,
  MISS DARDY's developing charms,
And agreed to tag on to his own,
  Her name and her newly-found arms.

The waiter he knelt at the toes
  Of an ugly and thin coryphée,
Who danced in the hindermost rows
  At the Théatre des Variétés.

MADEMOISELLE DE LA SAUCE MAYONNAISE
  Didn't yield to a gnawing despair
But married a soldier, and plays
  As a pretty and pert Vivandière.

BABETTE'S LOVE

BABETTE she was a fisher gal,
　　With jupon striped and cap in crimps,
She passed her days inside the Halle,
　　Or catching little nimble shrimps.
Yet she was sweet as flowers in May,
With no professional bouquet.

JACOT was, of the Customs bold,
　　An officer, at gay Boulogne,
He loved BABETTE—his love he told,
　　And sighed, "Oh, soyez vous my own!"
But "Non!" said she, "JACOT, my pet,
Vous êtes trop scraggy pour BABETTE.

"Of one alone I nightly dream,
　　An able mariner is he,
And gaily serves the Gen'ral Steam-
　　Boat Navigation Companee.
I'll marry him, if he but will—
His name, I rather think, is BILL.

"I see him when he's not aware,
　　Upon our hospitable coast,

Reclining with an easy air
  Upon the *Port* against a post,
A-thinking of, I'll dare to say,
His native Chelsea far away!"

"Oh, mon!" exclaimed the Customs bold,
  "Mes yeux!" he said (which means "my eye")
"Oh, chère!" he also cried, I'm told,
  "Par Jove," he added, with a sigh.
"Oh, mon! oh, chère! mes yeux! par Jove!
Je n'aime pas cet enticing cove!"

The *Panther's* captain stood hard by,
  He was a man of morals strict
If e'er a sailor winked his eye,
  Straightway he had that sailor licked,
Mast-headed all (such was his code)
Who dashed or jiggered, blessed or blowed.

He wept to think a tar of his
  Should lean so gracefully on posts,
He sighed and sobbed to think of this,
  On foreign, French, and friendly coasts.
"It's human natur', p'raps—if so,
Oh, isn't human natur' low!"

He called his BILL, who pulled his curl,
  He said, "My BILL, I understand

BABETTE'S LOVE

You've captivated some young gurl
   On this here French and foreign land.
Her tender heart your beauties jog—
They do, you know they do, you dog.

"You have a graceful way, I learn,
   Of leaning airily on posts,
By which you've been and caused to burn
   A tender flame on these here coasts.
A fisher gurl, I much regret—
Her age, sixteen—her name, BABETTE.

"You'll marry her, you gentle tar—
   Your union I myself will bless,
And when you matrimonied are,
   I will appoint her stewardess."
But WILLIAM hitched himself and sighed,
And cleared his throat, and thus replied:

"Not so: unless you're fond of strife,
   You'd better mind your own affairs,
I have an able-bodied wife
   Awaiting me at Wapping Stairs;
If all this here to her I tell,
She'll larrup you and me as well.

"Skin-deep, and valued at a pin,
   Is beauty such as Venus owns—
Her beauty is beneath her skin,
   And lies in layers on her bones.
The other sailors of the crew
They always calls her 'Whopping Sue'!"

"Oho!" the Captain said, "I see!
   And is she then so very strong?"
"She'd take your honour's scruff," said he,
   "And pitch you over to Boulong!"
"I pardon you," the Captain said,
"The fair BABETTE you needn't wed."

Perhaps the Customs had his will,
   And coaxed the scornful girl to wed,
Perhaps the Captain and his BILL,
   And WILLIAM's little wife are dead;
Or p'raps they're all alive and well:
I cannot, cannot, cannot tell.

TO MY BRIDE

(WHOEVER SHE MAY BE)

OH! little maid!—(I do not know your name,
  Or who you are, so, as a safe precaution
I'll add)—Oh, buxom widow! married dame!
  (As one of these must be your present portion)
    Listen, while I unveil prophetic lore for you,
    And sing the fate that Fortune has in store for you.

You'll marry soon—within a year or twain—
  A bachelor of *circa* two-and-thirty,
Tall, gentlemanly, but extremely plain,
  And, when you're intimate, you call him "BERTIE."
    Neat—dresses well; his temper has been classified
    As hasty; but he's very quickly pacified.

You'll find him working mildly at the Bar,
  After a touch at two or three professions,
From easy affluence extremely far,
  A brief or two on Circuit—"soup" at Sessions;
    A pound or two from whist and backing horses,
    And, say three hundred from his own resources.

Quiet in harness; free from serious vice,
　His faults are not particularly shady,
You'll never find him *"shy"*—for, once or twice
　　Already, he's been driven by a lady,
　　　Who parts with him—perhaps a poor excuse for him—
　　　Because she hasn't any further use for him.

Oh! bride of mine—tall, dumpy, dark, or fair!
　Oh! widow—wife, maybe, or blushing maiden,
I've told *your* fortune; solved the gravest care
　　With which your mind has hitherto been laden.
　　　I've prophesied correctly, never doubt it;
　　　Now tell me mine—and please be quick about it!

You—only you—can tell me, an' you will,
　To whom I'm destined shortly to be mated,
Will she run up a heavy *modiste's* bill?
　　If so, I want to hear her income stated
　　　(This is a point which interests me greatly).
　　　To quote the bard, "Oh! have I seen her lately?"

Say, must I wait till husband number one
　Is comfortably stowed away at Woking?
How is her hair most usually done?
　　And tell me, please, will she object to smoking?
　　　The colour of her eyes, too, you may mention:
　　　Come, Sibyl, prophesy—I'm all attention.

SIR MACKLIN

Of all the youths I ever saw
  None were so wicked, vain, or silly,
So lost to shame and Sabbath law
  As worldly Tom, and Bob, and Billy.

For every Sabbath day they walked
  (Such was their gay and thoughtless natur')
In parks or gardens, where they talked
  From three to six, or even later.

Sir Macklin was a priest severe
  In conduct and in conversation,
It did a sinner good to hear
  Him deal in ratiocination.

He could in every action show
  Some sin, and nobody could doubt him.
He argued high, he argued low,
  He also argued round about him.

He wept to think each thoughtless youth
  Contained of wickedness a skinful,
And burnt to teach the awful truth,
  That walking out on Sunday's sinful.

"Oh, youths," said he, "I grieve to find
  The course of life you've been and hit on—
Sit down," said he, "and never mind
  The pennies for the chairs you sit on.

"My opening head is 'Kensington,'
  How walking there the sinner hardens,
Which when I have enlarged upon,
  I go to 'Secondly'—its 'Gardens.'

"My 'Thirdly' comprehendeth 'Hyde,'
  Of Secresy the guilts and shameses;
My 'Fourthly'—'Park'—its verdure wide—
  My 'Fifthly' comprehends 'St. James's.'

"That matter settled I shall reach
  The 'Sixthly' in my solemn tether,
And show that what is true of each,
  Is also true of all, together.

"Then I shall demonstrate to you,
  According to the rules of Whately,
That what is true of all, is true
  Of each, considered separately."

SIR MACKLIN

In lavish stream his accents flow,
 TOM, BOB, and BILLY dare not flout him;
He argued high, he argued low,
 He also argued round about him.

"Ha, ha!" he said, "you loathe your ways,
 Repentance on your souls is dawning,
In agony your hands you raise."
 (And so they did, for they were yawning.)

To "Twenty-firstly" on they go,
 The lads do not attempt to scout him;
He argued high, he argued low,
 He also argued round about him.

"Ho, ho!" he cries, "you bow your crests—
 My eloquence has set you weeping;

In shame you bend upon your breasts!"
  (And so they did, for they were sleeping.)

He proved them this—he proved them that—
  This good but wearisome ascetic;
He jumped and thumped upon his hat,
  He was so very energetic.

His Bishop at this moment chanced
  To pass, and found the road encumbered;
He noticed how the Churchman danced,
  And how his congregation slumbered.

The hundred and eleventh head
  The priest completed of his stricture;
"Oh, bosh!" the worthy bishop said,
  And walked him off, as in the picture.

THE YARN OF THE "NANCY BELL"

'Twas on the shores that round our coast
　　From Deal to Ramsgate span,
That I found alone on a piece of stone
　　An elderly naval man.

His hair was weedy, his beard was long,
　　And weedy and long was he,
And I heard this wight on the shore recite,
　　In a singular minor key:

"Oh, I am a cook and a captain bold,
　　And the mate of the *Nancy* brig,
And a bo'sun tight, and a midshipmite,
　　And the crew of the captain's gig."

And he shook his fists and he tore his hair,
　　Till I really felt afraid,
For I couldn't help thinking the man had been drinking,
　　And so I simply said:

"Oh, elderly man, it's little I know
　　Of the duties of men of the sea,
And I'll eat my hand if I understand
　　However you can be

191

"At once a cook, and a captain bold,
And the mate of the *Nancy* brig,
And a bo'sun tight, and a midshipmite,
And the crew of the captain's gig."

Then he gave a hitch to his trousers, which
Is a trick all seamen larn,
And having got rid of a thumping quid,
He spun this painful yarn:

" 'Twas in the good ship *Nancy Bell*
That we sailed to the Indian Sea,
And there on a reef we come to grief,
Which has often occurred to me.

"And pretty nigh all the crew was drowned
(There was seventy-seven o' soul),
And only ten of the *Nancy's* men
Said 'Here!' to the muster-roll.

"There was me and the cook and the captain bold,
And the mate of the *Nancy* brig,
And the bo'sun tight, and a midshipmite,
And the crew of the captain's gig.

"For a month we'd neither wittles nor drink,
Till a-hungry we did feel,
So we drawed a lot, and, accordin' shot
The captain for our meal.

"The next lot fell to the *Nancy's* mate,
And a delicate dish he made;
And then our appetite with the midshipmite
We seven survivors stayed.

"And then we murdered the bo'sun tight,
And he much resembled pig;
Then we wittled free, did the cook and me,
On the crew of the captain's gig.

"Then only the cook and me was left,
  And the delicate question, 'Which
Of us two goes to the kettle?' arose
  And we argued it out as sich.

"For I loved that cook as a brother, I did,
  And the cook he worshipped me;
But we'd both be blowed if we'd either be stowed
  In the other chap's hold, you see.

" 'I'll be eat if you dines off me,' says Tom,
  'Yes, that,' says I, 'you'll be,'—
'I'm boiled if I die, my friend,' quoth I,
  And 'Exactly so,' quoth he.

"Says he, 'Dear James, to murder me
  Were a foolish thing to do,
For don't you see that you can't cook *me*,
  While I can—and will—cook *you!*'

"So he boils the water, and takes the salt
  And the pepper in portions true
(Which he never forgot), and some chopped shalot,
  And some sage and parsley too.

" 'Come here,' says he, with a proper pride,
  Which his smiling features tell,
' 'Twill soothing be if I let you see
  How extremely nice you'll smell.'

"And he stirred it round and round and round,
  And he sniffed at the foaming froth;
When I ups with his heels, and smothers his squeals
  In the scum of the boiling broth.

"And I eat that cook in a week or less,
  And—as I eating be
The last of his chops, why, I almost drops,
  For a wessel in sight I see!

*   *   *   *   *   *   *

"And I never larf, and I never smile,
  And I never lark nor play,
But sit and croak, and a single joke
  I have—which is to say:

" 'Oh, I am a cook and a captain bold,
  And the mate of the *Nancy* brig,
And a bo'sun tight, and a midshipmite,
  And the crew of the captain's gig!' "

THE BISHOP OF RUM-TI-FOO

FROM east and south the holy clan
Of Bishops gathered, to a man;
To Synod, called Pan-Anglican,
    In flocking crowds they came.
Among them was a Bishop, who
Had lately been appointed to
The balmy isle of Rum-ti-Foo,
    And PETER was his name.

His people—twenty-three in sum—
They played the eloquent tum-tum,
And lived on scalps served up in rum—
    The only sauce they knew.
When first good Bishop PETER came
(For PETER was that Bishop's name),
To humour them, he did the same
    As they of Rum-ti-Foo.

His flock, I've often heard him tell,
(His name was PETER) loved him well,
And summoned by the sound of bell,
    In crowds together came.

"Oh, massa, why you go away?
Oh, Massa PETER, please to stay."
(They called him PETER, people say,
    Because it was his name.)

He told them all good boys to be,
And sailed away across the sea,
At London Bridge that Bishop he
    Arrived one Tuesday night—
And as forthwith he homeward strode
To his Pan-Anglican abode,
He passed along the Borough Road
    And saw a gruesome sight.

He saw a crowd assembled round
A person dancing on the ground,
Who straight began to leap and bound
    With all his might and main.

To see that dancing man he stopped,
Who twirled and wriggled, skipped and hopped,
Then down incontinently dropped,
    And then sprang up again.

The Bishop chuckled at the sight,
"This style of dancing would delight
A simple Rum-ti-Foozleite,
    I'll learn it if I can,
To please the tribe when I get back."
He begged the man to teach his knack.

"Right Reverend Sir, in half a crack,"
    Replied that dancing man.

The dancing man he worked away,
And taught the Bishop every day—
The dancer skipped like any fay—
    Good PETER did the same.
The Bishop buckled to his task,
With *battements,* and *pas de basque.*
(I'll tell you, if you care to ask,
    That PETER was his name.)

"Come, walk like this," the dancer said,
"Stick out your toes—stick in your head,
Stalk on with quick, galvanic tread—
    Your fingers thus extend;

The attitude's considered quaint."
The weary Bishop, feeling faint,
Replied, "I do not say it ain't,
    But 'Time!' my Christian friend!"

"We now proceed to something new—
Dance as the PAYNES and LAURIS do,
Like this—one, two—one, two—one, two."
    The Bishop, never proud,
But in an overwhelming heat
(His name was PETER, I repeat)
Performed the PAYNE and LAURI feat,
    And puffed his thanks aloud.

Another game the dancer planned—
"Just take your ankle in your hand,
And try, my lord, if you can stand—
    Your body stiff and stark.
If, when revisiting your see,
You learnt to hop on shore—like me—
The novelty would striking be,
    And must attract remark."

"No," said the worthy Bishop, "No;
That is a length to which, I trow,
Colonial Bishops cannot go.
    You may express surprise
At finding Bishops deal in pride—
But, if that trick I ever tried,
I should appear undignified
    In Rum-ti-Foozle's eyes.

"The islanders of Rum-ti-Foo
Are well-conducted persons, who
Approve a joke as much as you,
    And laugh at it as such;
But if they saw their Bishop land,
His leg supported in his hand,
The joke they wouldn't understand—
    'Twould pain them very much!"

THE PRECOCIOUS BABY

A VERY TRUE TALE.

(To be sung to the air of the "Whistling Oyster.")

An elderly person—a prophet by trade—
    With his quips and tips
    On withered old lips,
He married a young and a beautiful maid;
    The cunning old blade!
    Though rather decayed,
He married a beautiful, beautiful maid.

She was only eighteen, and as fair as could be,
    With her tempting smiles
    And maidenly wiles,
And he was a trifle past seventy-three:
    Now what she could see
    Is a puzzle to me,
In a prophet of seventy—seventy-three!

Of all their acquaintances bidden (or bad)
    With their loud high jinks
    And underbred winks,

None thought they'd a family have—but they had;
>> A dear little lad
>> Who drove 'em half mad,
For he turned out a horribly fast little cad.

For when he was born he astonished all by,
>> With their "Law, dear me!"
>> "Did ever you see."
He'd a weed in his mouth and a glass in his eye,
>> A hat all awry—
>> An octagon tie,
And a miniature—miniature glass in his eye.

He grumbled at wearing a frock and a cap,
>> With his "Oh dear, no!"
>> And his "Hang it! 'oo know!"
And he turned up his nose at his excellent pap—
>> "My friends, it's a tap
>> Dat is not worf a rap."
(Now this was remarkably excellent pap.)

THE PRECOCIOUS BABY

He'd chuck his nurse under the chin, and he'd say,
    With his "Fal, lal, lal"—
    " 'Oo doosed fine gal!"
This shocking precocity drove 'em away:
    "A month from to-day
    Is as long as I'll stay—
Then I'd wish, if you please, for to go, if I may."

His father, a simple old gentleman, he
    With nursery rhyme
    And "Once on a time,"
Would tell him the story of "Little Bo-P,"
    "So pretty was she,
    So pretty and wee,
As pretty, as pretty, as pretty could be."

But the babe, with a dig that would startle an ox,
    With his "C'ck! Oh, my!—
    Go along wiz 'oo, fie!"
Would exclaim, "I'm affaid 'oo a socking ole fox."
    Now a father it shocks,
    And it whitens his locks,
When his little babe calls him a shocking old fox.

The name of his father he'd couple and pair
    (With his ill-bred laugh,
    And insolent chaff)
With those of the nursery heroines rare—
    Virginia the Fair,
    Or Good Goldenhair,
Till the nuisance was more than a prophet could bear.

"There's Jill and White Cat" (said the bold little brat,
    With his loud "Ha, ha!")
    " 'Oo sly ickle pa!
Wiz 'oo Beauty, Bo-Peep, and 'oo Mrs. Jack Sprat!
    I've noticed 'oo pat
    My pretty White Cat—
I sink dear mamma ought to know about dat!"

He early determined to marry and wive,
        For better or worse
        With his elderly nurse—
Which the poor little boy didn't live to contrive:
        His health didn't thrive—
        No longer alive,
He died an enfeebled old dotard at five!

Now, elderly men of the bachelor crew,
        With wrinkled hose
        And spectacled nose,
Don't marry at all—you may take it as true
        If ever you do
        The step you will rue,
For your babes will be elderly—elderly too.

TO PHŒBE

"Gentle, modest, little flower,
   Sweet epitome of May,
Love me but for half-an-hour,
   Love me, love me, little fay."
Sentences so fiercely flaming
   In your tiny shell-like ear,
I should always be exclaiming
   If I loved you, Phœbe, dear.

"Smiles that thrill from any distance
   Shed upon me while I sing!
Please ecstaticise existence,
   Love me, oh thou fairy thing!"
Words like these, outpouring sadly,
   You'd perpetually hear,
If I loved you, fondly, madly;—
   But I do not, Phœbe, dear.

THOMAS WINTERBOTTOM HANCE

In all the towns and cities fair
  On Merry England's broad expanse,
No swordsman ever could compare
  With Thomas Winterbottom Hance.

The dauntless lad could fairly hew
  A silken handkerchief in twain,
Divide a leg of mutton too—
  And this without unwholesome strain.

On whole half-sheep, with cunning trick,
  His sabre sometimes he'd employ—
No bar of lead, however thick,
  Had terrors for the stalwart boy.

At Dover daily he'd prepare
  To hew and slash, behind, before—
Which aggravated Monsieur Pierre,
  Who watched him from the Calais shore.

It caused good Pierre to swear and dance,
  The sight annoyed and vexed him so;

He was the bravest man in France—
  He said so, and he ought to know.

"Regardez donc, ce cochon gros—
  Ce polisson! Oh, sacré bleu!
Son sabre, son plomb, et ses gigots!
  Comme cela m'ennuye, enfin, mon Dieu!

"Il sait que les foulards de soie
  Give no retaliating whack—
Les gigots morts n'ont pas de quoi—
  Le plomb don't ever hit you back."

But every day the zealous lad
  Cut lead and mutton more and more;
And every day, poor PIERRE, half mad,
  Shrieked loud defiance from his shore.

HANCE had a mother, poor and old,
  A simple, harmless village dame,
Who crowed and clapped as people told
  Of WINTERBOTTOM's rising fame.

She said, "I'll be upon the spot
  To see my TOMMY's sabre-play";
And so she left her leafy cot,
  And walked to Dover in a day.

205

Pierre had a doting mother, who
　Had heard of his defiant rage:
His ma was nearly eighty-two,
　And rather dressy for her age.

At Hance's doings every morn,
　With sheer delight *his* mother cried;
And Monsieur Pierre's contemptuous scorn
　Filled *his* mamma with proper pride.

But Hance's powers began to fail—
　His constitution was not strong—
And Pierre, who once was stout and hale,
　Grew thin from shouting all day long.

Their mothers saw them pale and wan,
　Maternal anguish tore each breast,
And so they met to find a plan
　To set their offsprings' minds at rest.

Said Mrs. Hance, "Of course I shrinks
　From bloodshed, ma'am, as you're aware,
But still they'd better meet, I thinks."
　"Assurément!" said Madame Pierre.

A sunny spot in sunny France
　Was hit upon for this affair;
The ground was picked by Mrs. Hance,
　The stakes were pitched by Madame Pierre.

Said Mrs. H., "Your work you see—
Go in, my noble boy, and win."
"En garde, mon fils!" said Madame P.
"Allons!" "Go on!" "En garde!" "Begin!"

(The mothers were of decent size,
Though not particularly tall;
But in the sketch that meets your eyes
I've been obliged to draw them small.)

Loud sneered the doughty man of France,
"Ho! ho! Ho! ho! Ha! ha! Ha! ha!"
"The French for 'Pish!'" said Thomas Hance.
Said Pierre, "L'Anglais, Monsieur, pour 'Bah.'"

Said Mrs. H., "Come, one! two! three!—
We're sittin' here to see all fair."
"C'est magnifique!" said Madame P.,
"Mais, parbleu! ce n'est pas la guerre!"

"Je scorn un foe si lâche que vous,"
Said Pierre, the doughty son of France.
"I fight not coward foe like you!"
Said our undaunted Tommy Hance.

W. S. GILBERT

"The French for 'Pooh!'" our TOMMY cried.
"L'Anglais pour 'Va!'" the Frenchman crowed.
And so, with undiminished pride,
Each went on his respective road.

THE GHOST, THE GALLANT, THE GAEL,
AND THE GOBLIN

O'ER unreclaimed suburban clays
  Some years ago were hobblin'
An elderly ghost of easy ways,
  And an influential goblin.
The ghost was a sombre spectral shape,
  A fine old five-act fogy,
The goblin imp, a lithe young ape,
  A fine low-comedy bogy.

And as they exercised their joints,
  Promoting quick digestion,
They talked on several curious points,
  And raised this pregnant question:
"Which of us two is Number One—
  The ghostie, or the goblin?"
And o'er the point they raised in fun
  They fairly fell a-squabblin'.

They'd barely speak, and each, in fine,
  Grew more and more reflective,
Each thought his own particular line
  By far the more effective.

At length they settled some one should
  By each of them be haunted,
And so arranged that either could
  Exert his prowess vaunted.

"The Quaint against the Statuesque"—
  By competition lawful—
The goblin backed the Quaint Grotesque,
  The ghost the Grandly Awful.
"Now," said the goblin, "here's my plan—
  In attitude commanding,
I see a stalwart Englishman
  By yonder tailor's standing.

"The very fittest man on earth
  My influence to try on—
Of gentle, p'raps of noble birth,
  And dauntless as a lion!
Now wrap yourself within your shroud—
  Remain in easy hearing—
Observe—you'll hear him scream aloud
  When I begin appearing!"

The imp with yell unearthly—wild—
  Threw off his dark enclosure:
His dauntless victim looked and smiled
  With singular composure.
For hours he tried to daunt the youth,
  For days, indeed, but vainly—
The stripling smiled!—to tell the truth,
  The stripling smiled inanely.

For weeks the goblin weird and wild,
  That noble stripling haunted;
For weeks the stripling stood and smiled,
  Unmoved and all undaunted.
The sombre ghost exclaimed, "Your plan
  Has failed you, goblin, plainly:
Now watch yon hardy Hieland man,
  So stalwart and ungainly.

"These are the men who chase the roe,
 Whose footsteps never falter,
Who bring with them where'er they go,
 A smack of old SIR WALTER.
Of such as he, the men sublime
 Who lead their troops victorious,
Whose deeds go down to after-time,
 Enshrined in annals glorious!

"Of such as he the bard has said
 'Hech thrawfu' raltie rawkie!
Wi' thecht ta' croonie clapperhead
 And fash' wi' unco pawkie!'
He'll faint away when I appear
 Upon his native heather;
Or p'raps he'll only scream with fear,
 Or p'raps the two together."

The spectre showed himself, alone,
 To do his ghostly battling,
With curdling groan and dismal moan
 And lots of chains a-rattling!

But no—the chiel's stout Gaelic stuff
 Withstood all ghostly harrying,
His fingers closed upon the snuff
 Which upwards he was carrying.

For days that ghost declined to stir,
 A foggy shapeless giant—
For weeks that splendid officer
 Stared back again defiant.
Just as the Englishman returned
 The goblin's vulgar staring,
Just so the Scotchman boldly spurned
 The ghost's unmannered scaring.

For several years the ghostly twain
 These Britons bold have haunted,
But all their efforts are in vain—
 Their victims stand undaunted.
Unto this day the imp and ghost
 (Whose powers the imp derided)
Stand each at his allotted post—
 The bet is undecided.

KING BORRIA BUNGALEE BOO

King Borria Bungalee Boo
  Was a man-eating African swell;
His sigh was a hullabaloo,
  His whisper a horrible yell—
  A horrible, horrible yell!

Four subjects, and all of them male,
  To Borria doubled the knee,
They were once on a far larger scale,
  But he'd eaten the balance, you see
  ("Scale" and "balance" is punning, you see).

There was haughty Pish-Tush-Pooh-Bah,
  There was lumbering Doodle-Dum-Dey,
Despairing Alack-a-Dey-Ah,
  And good little Tootle-Tum-Teh—
  Exemplary Tootle-Tum-Teh.

One day there was grief in the crew,
  For they hadn't a morsel of meat,
And Borria Bungalee Boo
  Was dying for something to eat—
  "Come, provide me with something to eat!

"ALACK-A-DEY, famished I feel;
  Oh, good little TOOTLE-TUM-TEH,
Where on earth shall I look for a meal?
  For I haven't no dinner to-day!—
  Not a morsel of dinner to-day!

"Dear TOOTLE-TUM, what shall we do?
  Come, get us a meal, or in truth,
If you don't we shall have to eat you,
  Oh, adorable friend of our youth!
  Thou beloved little friend of our youth!"

And he answered, "Oh, BUNGALEE BOO,
  For a moment I hope you will wait,—
TIPPY-WIPPITY TOL-THE-ROL-LOO
  Is the Queen of a neighbouring state—
  A remarkably neighbouring state.

"TIPPY-WIPPITY TOL-THE-ROL-LOO,
  She would pickle deliciously cold—
And her four pretty Amazons, too,
  Are enticing, and not very old—
  Twenty-seven is not very old.

"There is neat little TITTY-FOL-LEH,
  There is rollicking TRAL-THE-RAL-LAH,

There is jocular WAGGETY-WEH,
　There is musical DOH-REH-MI-FAH—
　There's the nightingale DOH-REH-MI-FAH!"

So the forces of BUNGALEE BOO
　Marched forth in a terrible row,
And the ladies who fought for QUEEN LOO
　Prepared to encounter the foe—
　This dreadful insatiate foe!

But they sharpened no weapons at all,
　And they poisoned no arrows—not they!
They made ready to conquer or fall

　　In a totally different way—
　　An entirely different way.

With a crimson and pearly-white dye
　They endeavoured to make themselves fair,
With black they encircled each eye,
　And with yellow they painted their hair
　(It was wool, but they thought it was hair).

And the forces they met in the field:—
　And the men of KING BORRIA said,
"Amazonians, immediately yield!"
　And their arrows they drew to the head—
　Yes, drew them right up to the head.

But jocular WAGGETY-WEH
  Ogled DOODLE-DUM-DEY (which was wrong),
And neat little TITTY-FOL-LEH
  Said, "TOOTLE-TUM, you go along!
  You naughty old dear, go along!"

And rollicking TRAL-THE-RAL-LAH
  Tapped ALACK-A-DEY-AH with her fan;
And musical DOH-REH-MI-FAH
  Said, "PISH, go away, you bad man!
  Go away, you delightful young man!"

And the Amazons simpered and sighed,
  And they ogled, and giggled, and flushed,
And they opened their pretty eyes wide,
  And they chuckled, and flirted, and blushed
  (At least, if they could, they'd have blushed).

But haughty PISH-TUSH-POOH-BAH
  Said, "ALACK-A-DEY, what does this mean?"
And despairing ALACK-A-DEY-AH
  Said, "They think us uncommonly green—
  Ha! ha! most uncommonly green!"

Even blundering DOODLE-DUM-DEH
  Was insensible quite to their leers,
And said good little TOOTLE-TUM-TEH,
  "It's your blood that we're wanting, my dears—
  We have come for our dinners, my dears!"

And the Queen of the Amazons fell
  To BORRIA BUNGALEE BOO,—
In a mouthful he gulped, with a yell,
  TIPPY-WIPPY TOL-THE-ROL-LOO—
  The pretty QUEEN TOL-THE-ROL-LOO.

And neat little TITTY-FOL-LEH
  Was eaten by PISH-POOH-BAH,
And light-hearted WAGGETY-WEH
  By dismal ALACK-A-DEY-AH—
  Despairing ALACK-A-DEY-AH.

And rollicking Tral-the-Ral-Lah
　　Was eaten by Doodle-Dum-Dey,
And musical Doh-Reh-Mi-Fah
　　By good little Tootle-Tum-Teh—
　　Exemplary Tootle-Tum-Teh!

TO THE TERRESTRIAL GLOBE

BY A MISERABLE WRETCH

ROLL on, thou ball, roll on!
Through pathless realms of Space
  Roll on!
What though I'm in a sorry case?
What though I cannot meet my bills?
What though I suffer toothache's ills?
What though I swallow countless pills?
  Never *you* mind!
   Roll on!

Roll on, thou ball, roll on!
Through seas of inky air
  Roll on!
It's true I have no shirts to wear;
It's true my butcher's bill is due;
It's true my prospects all look blue—
But don't let that unsettle you!
  Never *you* mind!
   Roll on!

       [It rolls on.

GENTLE ALICE BROWN

It was a robber's daughter, and her name was Alice Brown,
Her father was the terror of a small Italian town;
Her mother was a foolish, weak, but amiable old thing;
But it isn't of her parents that I'm going for to sing.

As Alice was a-sitting at her window-sill one day,
A beautiful young gentleman he chanced to pass that way;
She cast her eyes upon him, and he looked so good and true,
That she thought, "I could be happy with a gentleman like you!"

And every morning passed her house that cream of gentlemen,
She knew she might expect him at a quarter unto ten,
A sorter in the Custom-house, it was his daily road
(The Custom-house was fifteen minutes' walk from her abode).

But Alice was a pious girl, who knew it wasn't wise
To look at strange young sorters with expressive purple eyes;
So she sought the village priest to whom her family confessed—
The priest by whom their little sins were carefully assessed.

"Oh, holy father," Alice said, "'twould grieve you, would it not?
To discover that I was a most disreputable lot!
Of all unhappy sinners I'm the most unhappy one!"
The padre said, "Whatever have you been and gone and done?"

"I have helped mamma to steal a little kiddy from its dad
I've assisted dear papa in cutting up a little lad.
I've planned a little burglary and forged a little cheque,
And slain a little baby for the coral on its neck!"

The worthy pastor heaved a sigh, and dropped a silent tear—
And said, "You mustn't judge yourself too heavily, my dear—
It's wrong to murder babies, little corals for to fleece;
But sins like these one expiates at half-a-crown apiece.

"Girls will be girls—you're very young, and flighty in your mind;
Old heads upon young shoulders we must not expect to find:
We mustn't be too hard upon these little girlish tricks—
Let's see—five crimes at half-a-crown—exactly twelve-and-six."

"Oh, father," little ALICE cried, "your kindness makes me weep,
You do these little things for me so singularly cheap—
Your thoughtful liberality I never can forget;
But oh, there is another crime I haven't mentioned yet!

"A pleasant-looking gentleman, with pretty purple eyes,
I've noticed at my window, as I've sat a-catching flies;
He passes by it every day as certain as can be—
I blush to say I've winked at him, and he has winked at me!"

"For shame!" said FATHER PAUL, "my erring daughter! On my word
This is the most distressing news that I have ever heard.
Why, naughty girl, your excellent papa has pledged your hand
To a promising young robber, the lieutenant of his band!

GENTLE ALICE BROWN

"This dreadful piece of news will pain your worthy parents so!
They are the most remunerative customers I know;
For many many years they've kept starvation from my doors:
I never knew so criminal a family as yours!

"The common country folk in this insipid neighbourhood
Have nothing to confess, they're so ridiculously good;
And if you marry any one respectable at all,
Why, you'll reform, and what will then become of FATHER PAUL?"

The worthy priest, he up and drew his cowl upon his crown,
And started off in haste to tell the news to ROBBER BROWN;
To tell him how his daughter, who was now for marriage fit,
Had winked upon a sorter, who reciprocated it.

Good ROBBER BROWN he muffled up his anger pretty well,
He said, "I have a notion, and that notion I will tell;
I will nab this gay young sorter, terrify him into fits,
And get my gentle wife to chop him into little bits.

"I've studied human nature, and I know a thing or two;
Though a girl may fondly love a living gent, as many do,
A feeling of disgust upon her senses there will fall
When she looks upon his body chopped particularly small."

He traced that gallant sorter to a still suburban square;
He watched his opportunity and seized him unaware;
He took a life-preserver and he hit him on the head,
And MRS. BROWN dissected him before she went to bed.

And pretty little ALICE grew more settled in her mind,
She never more was guilty of a weakness of the kind,
Until at length good ROBBER BROWN bestowed her pretty hand
On the promising young robber, the lieutenant of his band.

MY DREAM

THE other night, from cares exempt,
I slept—and what d'you think I dreamt?
I dreamt that somehow I had come
To dwell in Topsy-Turveydom!—

Where vice is virtue—virtue, vice:
Where nice is nasty—nasty, nice:
Where right is wrong and wrong is right—
Where white is black and black is white.

Where babies, much to their surprise,
Are born astonishingly wise;
With every Science on their lips,
And Art at all their finger-tips.

For, as their nurses dandle them,
They crow binomial theorem,
With views (it seems absurd to us)
On differential calculus.

But though a babe, as I have said,
Is born with learning in his head,
He must forget it, if he can,
Before he calls himself a man.

For that which we call folly here,
Is wisdom in that favoured sphere;
The wisdom we so highly prize
Is blatant folly in their eyes.

A boy, if he would push his way,
Must learn some nonsense every day;
And cut, to carry out this view,
His wisdom teeth and wisdom too.

Historians burn their midnight oils,
Intent on giant-killers' toils;
And sages close their aged eyes
To other sages' lullabies.

Our magistrates, in duty bound,
Commit all robbers who are found;
But there the beaks (so people said)
Commit all robberies instead.

Our judges, pure and wise in tone,
Know crime from theory alone,
And glean the motives of a thief
From books and popular belief.

But there, a Judge who wants to prime
His mind with true ideas of crime,
Derives them from the common sense
Of practical experience.

Policemen march all folks away
Who practise virtue every day—
Of course, I mean to say, you know,
What we call virtue here below.

For only scoundrels dare to do
What we consider just and true,
And only good men do, in fact,
What we should think a dirty act.

But strangest of these social twirls,
The girls are boys—the boys are girls!
The men are women, too—but then,
Per contra, women all are men.

To one who to tradition clings
This seems an awkward state of things,
But if to think it out you try,
It doesn't really signify.

With them, as surely as can be,
A sailor should be sick at sea,
And not a passenger may sail
Who cannot smoke right through a gale.

A soldier (save by rarest luck)
Is always shot for showing pluck

MY DREAM

(That is, if others can be found
With pluck enough to fire a round).

"How strange!" I said to one I saw;
"You quite upset our every law.
However can you get along
So systematically wrong?"

"Dear me," my mad informant said,
"Have you no eyes within your head?
You sneer when you your hat should doff:
Why, we begin where you leave off!

"Your wisest men are very far
Less learned than our babies are!"
I mused awhile—and then, oh me!
I framed this brilliant repartee:

"Although your babes are wiser far
Than our most valued sages are,
Your sages, with their toys and cots,
Are duller than our idiots!"

But this remark, I grieve to state,
Came just a little bit too late;
For as I framed it in my head,
I woke and found myself in bed.

Still I could wish that, 'stead of here,
My lot were in that favoured sphere!—
Where greatest fools bear off the bell
I ought to do extremely well.

THE FAIRY CURATE

ONCE a fairy
Light and airy
Married with a mortal;
   Men, however,
   Never, never
Pass the fairy portal.
   Slyly stealing,
   She to Ealing
Made a daily journey;
   There she found him,
   Clients round him
(He was an attorney).

   Long they tarried,
   Then they married.
When the ceremony
   Once was ended,
   Off they wended
On their moon of honey.
   Twelvemonth, maybe,
   Saw a baby

227

(Friends performed an orgie).
Much they prized him,
And baptized him
By the name of GEORGIE.

GEORGIE grew up;
Then he flew up
To his fairy mother.
Happy meeting
Pleasant greeting—
Kissing one another.
"Choose a calling
Most enthralling,
I sincerely urge ye."
"Mother," said he
(Rev'rence made he),
"I would join the clergy.

"Give permission
In addition—
Pa will let me do it:
There's a living
In his giving,
He'll appoint me to it.
Dreams of coff'ring
Easter off'ring,
Tithe and rent and pew-rate,
So inflame me
(Do not blame me),
That I'll be a curate."

She, with pleasure,
Said, "My treasure,
'Tis my wish precisely.
Do your duty,
There's a beauty;
You have chosen wisely.
Tell your father
I would rather

As a churchman rank you.
    You, in clover,
    I'll watch over."
GEORGIE said, "Oh, thank you!"

    GEORGIE scudded,
    Went and studied,
Made all preparations,
    And with credit
    (Though he said it)
Passed examinations.
    (Do not quarrel
    With him, moral,
Scrupulous digestions—
    'Twas his mother,
    And no other,
Answered all the questions.)

    Time proceeded;
    Little needed
GEORGIE admonition:
    He, elated,
    Vindicated
Clergyman's position.
    People round him
    Always found him
Plain and unpretending;
    Kindly teaching,
    Plainly preaching—
All his money lending.

    So the fairy,
    Wise and wary,
Felt no sorrow rising—
    No occasion
    For persuasion,
Warning, or advising.
    He, resuming
    Fairy pluming
(That's not English, is it?)

Oft would fly up,
To the sky up,
Pay mamma a visit.

*　　*　　*　　*

Time progressing,
GEORGIE's blessing
Grew more Ritualistic—
Popish scandals,
Tonsures—sandals—
Genuflections mystic;
Gushing meetings—
Bosom-beatings—
Heavenly ecstatics—
Broidered spencers—
Copes and censers—
Rochets and dalmatics.

230

This quandary
Vexed the fairy—
Flew she down to Ealing.
"GEORGIE, stop it!
Pray you, drop it;
Hark to my appealing:
To this foolish
Papal rule-ish
Twaddle put an ending;
This a swerve is
From our Service
Plain and unpretending."

He, replying,
Answered, sighing,
Hawing, hemming, humming,
"It's a pity—
They're so pritty;
Yet in mode becoming,
Mother tender,
I'll surrender—
I'll be unaffected——"
But his Bishop
Into *his* shop
Entered unexpected!

"Who is this, sir,—
Ballet miss, sir?"
Said the Bishop coldly.
" 'Tis my mother,
And no other,"
GEORGIE answered boldly.
"Go along, sir!
You are wrong, sir,
You have years in plenty;
While this hussy
(Gracious mussy!)
Isn't two-and-twenty!"

(Fairies clever
Never, never
Grow in visage older;
And the fairy,
All unwary,
Leant upon his shoulder!)
Bishop grieved him,
Disbelieved him,
GEORGE the point grew warm on;
Changed religion,
Like a pigeon,[1]
And became a Mormon.

[1] "Like a bird."